FIRST DOGS

FIRST DOGS

AMERICAN PRESIDENTS

& THEIR BEST FRIENDS

by Roy Rowan and Brooke Janis

Algonquin Books of Chapel Hill   2009

Published by

ALGONQUIN BOOKS OF CHAPEL HILL

Post Office Box 2225

Chapel Hill, North Carolina 27515-2225

a division of

WORKMAN PUBLISHING

225 Varick Street

New York, New York 10014

Printed in the United States of America.

Published simultaneously in Canada by Thomas Allen & Son Limited.

Library of Congress Cataloging-in-Publication Data

Rowan, Roy.

First dogs : American presidents and their best friends / by Roy Rowan
and Brooke Janis. — Expanded ed.

p. cm.

"Published simultaneously in Canada by Thomas Allen & Son" — T.p. verso.

ISBN 978-1-56512-936-8

1. Presidents — United States — Pets — Anecdotes.   2. Dogs — United
States — Anecdotes.   I. Janis, Brooke.   II. Title.

E176.48.R68 2009

636.70973 — dc22   2009017544

10   9   8   7   6   5   4   3   2

For Helen and for Lee,

without whom we'd have

gone to the dogs

CONTENTS

FIRST DOGS

A CABINET SEAT FOR LADDIE BOY

Warren Harding's airedale not only had his own hand-carved chair to sit in during Cabinet meetings, he had a personal White House valet. In a famous interview with The Washington Star, *Laddie Boy rated members of the President's Cabinet and offered opinions on such subjects as the working hours of guard dogs and the use of sled dogs to haul mail in Alaska.*

Ohio Historical Society

* * *

HAIL TO THE
CHIEF (DOG)

I F YOU WANT A FRIEND IN WASHINGTON," HARRY TRUMAN ONCE SAID, "GET A DOG." MAYBE THAT'S why for most of our Republic's history there have been two top dogs at 1600 Pennsylvania Avenue—one with two legs, one with four. However, never before the election of Barack Obama had the selection of a First Dog been anticipated with such excitement. From the moment of his victory speech before cheering thousands in Chicago, when he promised his two daughters that they could have a puppy in the White House, the picking of a First Dog was followed with the same rapt attention as the appointment of the new President's cabinet.

Occupants of the White House Oval Office, we all know, leave us their memoirs before passing from the scene. George H. W. Bush's springer spaniel, Millie, was no exception. *Millie's Book* was her own heart-warming account (as dictated to Barbara Bush) of a dog's life in the White House. But Millie's book ultimately proved

COLD WAR COUPLE

Welsh terrier Charlie and Russian mate Pushinka, happy as any newly-
weds, pose in front of the Kennedy White House. They produced four pups:
Butterfly, White Tips, Blackie, and Streaker. John F. Kennedy Library

* * *

to be something of an embarrassment to the President, outselling his own memoirs. And her stature as a bestselling author did not succeed in helping him defeat the dogless Bill Clinton in 1992.

For the first five years under Clinton the White House was the domain of a white-pawed cat named Socks. But one of the dark secrets of Bill Clinton's days as governor of Arkansas concerns the mysterious death of Zeke. The cute blond cocker spaniel somehow escaped from the governor's mansion and was run over by a car several years before Clinton's 1992 presidential bid. Zeke was often seen cavorting around the governor's mansion in Little Rock along with Bill, Hillary, and Chelsea. He starred in various photo ops, especially the one accompanying the proclamation of Be Kind to Animals Week. The circumstances surrounding his death are unclear, and so far the Whitewater Special Counsel has not investigated them. Given what practically amounted to a state funeral, Zeke presently rests in peace behind the Arkansas governor's mansion.

By coming dogless to the White House, Clinton was defying not only tradition, but also the warning of a former chief executive. "Any man who does not like dogs and want them about," claimed Calvin Coolidge, "does not deserve to be in the White House."

Many Americans seem to have shared Coolidge's view. Since

the first days of the Union, our presidents have been measured in part by the canine company they kept. In fact, some presidential dogs, like Franklin Delano Roosevelt's Fala, appeared to have wagged the tail of U.S. policy.

Fala and FDR were inseparable, their lives intertwined with the World War II history of our country. Yet this Scottie celebrity was a canine nobody named Big Boy, watering trees and burying bones in Westport, Connecticut, before he was presented to Roosevelt. Renamed Murray the Outlaw of Fala Hill after one of the President's Scottish ancestors, he is now buried beside his master in the Rose Garden at Roosevelt's Hyde Park, New York, estate.

What an extraordinary life this little dog led! He witnessed the signing of the Atlantic Charter aboard the USS *Augusta*, becoming a shipboard pal of British prime minister Winston Churchill's poodle Rufus. He often rode in the limo beside Roosevelt past cheering crowds lining Pennsylvania Avenue. And, so the story goes, Roosevelt ordered a destroyer sent back to fetch Fala after he was mistakenly left behind in the Aleutian Islands. Political opponents carped that this naval rescue operation had cost American taxpayers $15,000. "These Republicans have not been content with attacks on me, my wife, or my sons," exclaimed Roosevelt in one of his famous fireside chats. "No, not content with that, they now include my little dog, Fala."

THE EAR-IE STORY OF HIM AND HER

*Irate dog lovers demanded an explanation when Lyndon Johnson picked up
his beagles, Him and Her, by their ears. "To make them bark," replied LBJ.
"It's good for them." The two beagles' White House days ended sadly. Her died
on the operating table after swallowing a rock. Him was run over by a car while
chasing a squirrel across the White House driveway.* UPI/Corbis-Bettmann

NIXON'S CHECKERED CAREER

In 1952 the Eisenhower-Nixon ticket was far ahead in the polls when a story surfaced that Nixon had a secret slush fund contributed by rich supporters. His cocker spaniel Checkers was used to win public sympathy. If it hadn't been for this cute dog, Nixon's political career might have ended right there. The Richard Nixon Library & Birthplace

★ ★ ★

Canine diplomacy goes back to the very founding of the nation. Several of the hounds that George Washington rode to were French imports, which explains why they bore such sexy names as Sweet Lips and Scentwell. They were sent by Washington's Revolutionary War comrade the Marquis de Lafayette, who gave them to our country's founding father to cement relations between France and the newly independent United States. Years later, those same diplomatic ties needed a little patching, as did the striped pants of the French ambassador, after Teddy Roosevelt's bull terrier Pete chewed a hole in them at a White House reception.

Lafayette was not the only foreign leader to have used this canine approach for currying favor with the U.S. China's Empress Dowager Ci-Xi gave Teddy's young daughter Alice a tiny Oriental spaniel named Manchu. When U.S.-Soviet relations were at a low ebb following the Cuban missile crisis in 1962, Premier Nikita Khrushchev sought to reduce tensions between our two countries by presenting JFK's daughter, Caroline, with a fluffy white Russian mutt named Pushinka. Daughter of one of the USSR's famed space dogs, Pushinka was checked by the CIA for bugs (but not for fleas) before being given the run of the White House, where she promptly fell in love with Caroline's Welsh terrier Charlie. Not even the Cold War could keep them apart, or

MOST FAMOUS FIRST DOG, FDR'S FALA

*Having attended many official functions with his master, Franklin,
Fala knew how to stand at attention. The Scottie was a gift from the
President's cousin Margaret Suckley. He lived in the White House
from 1942 until Roosevelt's death in 1945.* FDR Library

* * *

prevent Pushinka from producing a litter of four "pupniks," as President Kennedy referred to them.

Some presidential dogs were given official positions or performed useful services during their master's term of office. Faithful, the powerful Newfoundland pup of Ulysses Grant's son, was appointed a White House steward in order to intimidate the servants, who the President suspected of poisoning his children's pets. A White House dog called Veto got his name when James Garfield wanted to remind the rambunctious Congress of 1881 that he might not sign all of the bills it passed, which he claimed amounted to "a revolution against the Constitution." An airedale named Laddie Boy posed with Warren Harding for a poster repeating his campaign pledge of "Back to Normalcy with Harding." What could be more normal than a president assuming his lofty duties with "man's best friend" at his side? As soon as Laddie Boy moved into the White House he was given his own hand-carved high-backed chair to sit in during cabinet meetings.

Gerald Ford used his frisky female golden retriever Liberty to break up Oval Office meetings that lasted too long. And Liberty was no lady when it came to helping her master stick to his tight schedule. The President simply whistled for the dog, who happily rushed in and pounced on those visitors overstaying their leave.

AUTHOR MILLIE ON HER MAINE VACATION

After summering in Maine and a year puttering around the vice president's official residence on the grounds of the U.S. Naval Observatory, Millie finally got to move into the White House with George and Barbara Bush. Her biography became a bestseller. But not all of Millie's media attention was favorable: she once appeared on the cover of Washingtonian *magazine after being voted D.C.'s "Ugliest Dog."* Bush Presidential Library

★ ★ ★

Some of the cutest dogs have also been used as foils to divert political blame. Early television viewers will remember how in 1952 vice-presidential candidate Richard Nixon, after being chastised for accepting gifts of $18,000, held up a small black-and-white cocker spaniel named Checkers in front of the cameras. "The kids love the dog," which he admitted was also a gift. "And we're gonna keep it!" exclaimed Nixon. He won instant sympathy, though he failed to mention whether he was going to keep the alleged gifts of money. Once he took over the Oval Office, Nixon chose a more regal-looking Irish setter, whom he named King Timahoe after a village in County Kildare from whence his ancestors hailed. "King," explained Nixon, "was added to the dog's name because if he's the presidential dog he'll be treated like a king, won't he?"

Not always. The way a president treats his dogs can be a source of considerable controversy. Lyndon Johnson was often pictured riding around Washington in his bulletproof limo with his twin beagles, Him and Her, beside him. But when he picked up the dogs by their long floppy ears, the countrywide howls of protest almost matched those set off by his escalation of the Vietnam War. And today, many people still remember Johnson holding his dogs up by their ears, and forget the Great Society, the Civil Rights Act, and the Johnson Space Center.

BILL, WITH THE LATE, LAMENTED ZEKE

Governor Clinton holds up his cocker spaniel during a photo op celebrating Arkansas Be Kind to Animals Week. Zeke, sadly, was run over before his master was elected president. But Clinton finally took Coolidge's advice and chose a chocolate Labrador retriever, whom he named Buddy, to share his final years in the Oval Office.

★ ★ ★

THE SQUIRE OF MONTICELLO

Thomas Jefferson forbade his slaves to keep dogs, though he kept them himself, as seen in this 1930 illustration by A. C. Wyatt. To a friend he wrote: "To secure wool enough, the negroes' dogs must all be killed." Wild dogs had become such a danger to the sheep that drastic action was necessary. But Jefferson worked assiduously to improve the breed of his briard sheepdogs. He wrote to a friend: "Besides their wonderful sagacity and never-ceasing attention to what they are taught to do, they appear to have more courage than I had before supposed that race to possess." Library of Congress

* * *

C H A P T E R   T W O

FOUNDING SIRES

GEORGE WASHINGTON
TO JOHN QUINCY ADAMS

DURING THE REVOLUTIONARY WAR, A HUNGRY HOUND OBVIOUSLY OF HIGH BREEDING wandered into General Washington's headquarters at Pennibecker's Mill near Germantown, Pennsylvania. The dog was lost and foraging for food, which was promptly provided. But a controversy quickly developed among the officers. Should they keep the dog for a mascot or turn it loose? Just then somebody noticed the name of General Howe, the British commander, engraved on the dog's collar. Washington settled the argument by proclaiming that the dog should be returned to its rightful owner under a white flag of truce. An avid fox hunter, the American commander understood the close bond between a man and his dog.

Historian Gary Wills has written that Washington "gained power by his willingness to give it up," and his decision to return Howe's dog seems entirely consistent with the way he surrendered his sword to Congress at the end of the war. He retreated to Mount Vernon to farm, raise livestock, and pursue his favorite sport of hunting foxes, which included the breeding of the hounds to chase them with.

Once elected president, however, he did not vacillate in exercising the authority vested in him by the voters, any more than he did in the strict training of his hunting dogs. He insisted on the president's sole authority over the Executive Branch. The chief executive would be rendered ineffective, claimed the squire of Mount Vernon, if prevented from being top dog.

Washington, a student of genetics and a breeder of hunting dogs, can be considered the father of the American foxhound as well as the father of our country. By crossing seven big stag hounds that the Marquis de Lafayette had given him with his own smaller black-and-tan Virginia hounds, he developed a new breed. His personal letters and detailed diaries reveal a desire to create "a superior dog, one that had speed, scent and brains." More than thirty hounds were listed by name in Washington's journals, including the wobbly-sounding trio of Drunkard, Tipler, and Tipsy.

The gift dogs from Lafayette resulted from a long correspondence with his old comrade-in-arms. The Marquis wrote in May 1785 that "French hounds are not Now Very Easely got Because

WASHINGTON WONDERED: WHERE OH
WHERE HAVE MY FRENCH DOGS GONE?

The seven French hounds sent to Washington by General Lafayette
were brought to America by young John Quincy Adams. For a while
Washington thought the dogs were missing and commented
disparagingly on the man who would become the country's sixth
president. Library of Congress

the King Makes use of English dogs as Being more Swift than those of Normandy." But Lafayette persevered. "I However Have got Seven from a Normand Cengleman Called Monsieur le Comte Doilliamson." The seven hounds were promptly dispatched to America aboard ship in the care of the young John Quincy Adams.

One of Washington's hopes was to breed Irish wolfhounds to protect his sheep. Sir Edward Newenham, whom he described as "a gentleman of family and fortune in Ireland," tried to help him. "I have been these several years endeavoring to get that breed without success," Sir Edward wrote. "It is nearly annihilated. I have heard of a bitch in northern Ireland but not of a couple anywhere." Washington then toyed with the idea of using mastiffs for this purpose, but found while they were good at guarding a sheep pen, they were "unfit to hunt and destroy wolves by pursuit." Eventually he gave up on the idea.

The other founding fathers, all of whom raised livestock, also complained of destructive dogs. Thomas Jefferson, author of the Declaration of Independence, originally disliked dogs because of the way they harassed and sometimes ate the sheep at Monticello. He once wrote to a friend, "I participate in all your hostility to dogs and would readily join in any plan of exterminating the whole race. I consider them the most afflicting of all follies for which men tax themselves."

An astute politician, Jefferson listened sympathetically to complaints about marauding hounds and came out publicly for enactment of a law "making the owner of a dog liable for all the mischief done by him, and requiring that every dog shall wear a collar with the name of the person inscribed who shall be security for his honest demeanor." Apparently the man who was to become the third president of the United States was also an originator of the dog license.

But while serving as minister to France, before being appointed Washington's Secretary of State, Jefferson became interested in the native sheepdogs. Known as the chien berger de Brie, the breed dated back to the days of Charlemagne. In 1789 Jefferson wrote to his assistant, William Short: "I was yesterday roving thro the neighborhood of this place to try to get a pair of shepherd's dogs. We walked ten miles clambering the cliffs in quest of the shepherds, during the most furious tempest of wind and rain I was ever in. The journey was fruitless." However, the next day he met with success and entered a notation in his Memorandum Book: "pd. for a chienne bergere big with pup, 36 Libre [the equivalent of six dollars], gratuity to the person who brought her, 9 [Libre]."

The next day he sailed for America, bringing the pregnant dog with him aboard the ship, *Clermont*. Apparently Bergere, or

HE NEVER LOOKED A GIFT DOG IN THE MOUTH

Hunting dogs and the game they tracked down littered Martha and George Washington's kitchen at Mount Vernon. Vulcan, the most mischievous of Washington's gift dogs from Lafayette, had an insatiable appetite. One evening, much to the delight of George and the dismay of his wife, Vulcan stole a freshly cooked Virginia ham from the place of honor at the dinner table and was said to have "run straight to the kennel with it locked in his great jaws." Library of Congress

★ ★ ★

Buzzy as she was later named, gave birth to two pups during the trans-Atlantic crossing, becoming the progenitor of an American line of briard-type sheepdogs. Jefferson was the recipient of two more briards, sent as a gift by Lafayette to assist in guarding his sheep at Monticello. Buzzy remained Jefferson's favorite. He described her many descendants as "remarkably quiet, faithful and abounding in the good qualities of the old bitch." But when one of the offspring was caught in the act of eating a sheep, it was summarily hanged.

Despite such harsh punishment, Jefferson in his old age described to his daughter Martha how for more than thirty years these "canine immigrants were carefully multiplied." He claimed he wanted to populate America with "the most careful, intelligent dogs in the world" and did much to improve the breed by placing the briards in pairs with other landholders. But Jefferson warned that these French dogs "must be reasonably fed; and are the better for being attached to a master. If they are forced by neglect and hunger to prowl for themselves, their sagacity renders them the most destructive marauders imaginable. You will see your flock of sheep and hogs disappearing from day to day, without ever being able to detect them in it. They learn readily to go for the cows of an evening or for the sheep, to drive up the ducks, turkies every one into their own house."

Jefferson lost his first try for the presidency in 1796. Branded an atheist, he was also accused of being an ardent friend of the French—providers of his beloved briards. His sixty-eight electoral votes, nevertheless, were enough to make him vice president in the administration of John Adams, who received seventy-one electoral votes.

Adams had the unenviable task of succeeding the revered Washington. Faced also with a divided cabinet and party, he returned to Massachusetts after one term in the White House. (He was the first president to live there.) His wife Abigail was happy to be back home, where she reported enjoying the companionship of her two dogs, Juno and Satan. The former First Lady wrote to her granddaughter Caroline Smith: "As if you love me proverbially, you must love my dog, you will be glad to learn that Juno yet lives, although like her mistress she is gray with age. She appears to enjoy life and to be grateful for the attention paid her. She wags her tail and announces a visiter [*sic*] whenever one appears."

In the hotly contested election of 1800, Jefferson and Aaron Burr received the same number of electoral votes. The House of Representatives then decided the outcome in favor of Jefferson, who campaigned as a Democratic-Republican to restore individual liberties and repeal Federalist policies aimed at turning the

A STRICT MASTER OF THE HOUNDS

Washington liked to ride off before breakfast on fox hunts with his hounds but complained that his dogs were "forever sustaining loss in my Stock of Sheep." He also forbade his slaves to keep dogs, fearing they would use the hounds for stealing things. He wrote to a friend: "If any Negro presumes under any pretence whatsoever, to preserve, or bring one into the family, he shall be severely punished and the dog hanged. . . . It is not for any good purpose Negroes raise or keep dogs, but to aid them in their night robberies, for it is astonishing to see the command under which their dogs are." Library of Congress

★ ★ ★

presidency into a monarchy. Neither Jefferson nor his three Democratic-Republican successors—James Madison, James Monroe, and John Quincy Adams—tried to enhance their influence through political patronage. As a result presidential power waned during their terms of office.

Presidential interest in dogs seemed to wane as well. Madison, a protégé of Jefferson's, did temporarily house a pair of his mentor's sheepdogs at his Montpelier estate in Virginia before sending them on by wagon to a friend in Washington. Monroe was also sent a pair of chien de Brie sheepdogs for his farm in Oak Hill, Virginia, by a grateful Lafayette. The President had helped the Marquis obtain a grant from Congress.

While he was president, Monroe's twelve-year-old daughter, Maria, had her own pet dog. A judge who visited the Monroes in Washington was so captivated by the girl that he wrote: "She had a small spaniel dog with whom she was continually engaged in a trial of skill—and the general opinion seemed to be that she turned and twisted about more than the spaniel."

John Quincy Adams, who had escorted the French hunting dogs across the Atlantic for George Washington, ultimately owned a dog himself. At least in 1817 he advertised in the newspaper for a lost dog, though it is not known whether it ever turned up. But during the four years of his rather unsuccessful presidency, there is no record of his having had one. His single term ended acrimoniously, with Congress and not the President in control of the government.

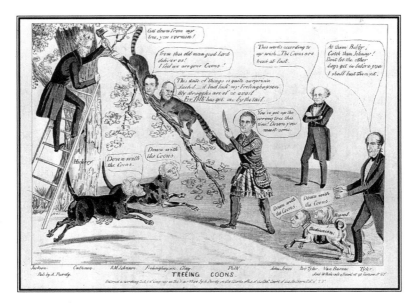

TYLER'S DOGS DON'T WIN THE DAY

Whig president John Tyler (extreme right), known as a lover of all animals, is shown in this 1844 election cartoon using his dogs to no avail. His Democratic opponent, James Polk, with a hunting knife in hand, already has one Whig coon, Henry Clay, by the tail, while former president Andrew Jackson assists Polk by chopping down the hickory limb that Clay and another Whig leader are trying to climb.

Library of Congress

★ ★ ★

CHAPTER THREE

DOGGED POPULISM

ANDREW JACKSON

TO JAMES POLK

ANDREW JACKSON—OR "OLD HICKORY," AS HE BECAME KNOWN—WAS A SELF-MADE MAN who rose from a small cabin in the piney woods of South Carolina to a plantation near Nashville and finally to the White House. As a country boy with little formal education, he doubtless grew up with dogs, most probably mutts, though there is no record of this. His love of dogs as president, however, was recorded in a letter to his new daughter-in-law, Sarah, in 1832. Fearing that his adopted son Andrew, Jr., might have become separated from his dog while the newlyweds were traveling to their home after a four month's stay in the White House, Jackson wrote: "I am truly glad to hear that Andrew has got safely on his fine dog. I was uneasy, as I knew his anxiety to have him lest he might be lost on the way. A dog is one of the most affectionate of all the animal species, and is worthy of regard, and Andrew's attachment for his dog is an evidence of the goodness of his heart."

Jackson, like Jefferson, prided himself on being a man of the people. In fact, the feelings evoked in that letter suggest not only an affection for dogs, but for his fellow man as well. He stood for the frontier principle of equality of opportunity—that no one should have special privileges at the expense of anyone else— which both enhanced his popularity as president and imposed on the young republic a new brand of democracy, which lasted for nearly three decades.

At the same time, the agrarian interests of the South and West were also triumphing over the commercial and financial interests of the East. These developments attracted farmers, laborers, and mechanics to the electorate—"the humble members of society," as Jackson called them. Their backing helped transform the presidency into a more powerful, popularly based office, at the expense of the Legislative Branch. In a further expansion of presidential power, Jackson initiated the "Spoils System" by which he replaced federal employees with political friends for purely partisan reasons.

Martin Van Buren, Jackson's politically shrewd successor and one of the few dogless occupants of the White House, was nevertheless vilified for allowing the War Department to employ

"CAUCUS CURS IN FULL YELL"

That was the title of a dog-filled cartoon criticizing Andrew Jackson's treatment by the press in the confusing 1824 presidential race won by John Quincy Adams. Jackson received the most electoral votes, Adams was second, and Republican Treasury Secretary William Crawford was third. Crawford then threw his support behind Adams, thus assuring his victory. Jackson, the hero of the Battle of New Orleans in the War of 1812, stands staunchly amid a pack of snarling dogs labeled with the names of the attacking newspapers. Secretary Crawford, who tipped the election in Adams's favor, stands beside the U.S. Treasury offering a bowl of dollars to a woman voter.

Library of Congress

* * *

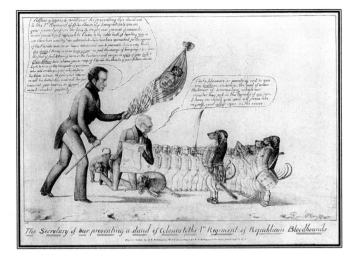

VAN BUREN'S REGIMENT OF BLOODHOUNDS

In this lithograph, Van Buren's Secretary of War, Joel Poinsett, presents the colors to a regiment of Republican bloodhounds used to track down Seminole Indians and remove them from their tribal lands in Florida. The furled flag bears the head of an Indian carried in the mouth of a dog. Newspaper editor Francis Preston Blair, an apologist for the Van Buren administration, is on his knees showing the bloodhounds a map of Florida. This was just one of several cartoons vilifying Van Buren for his cruelty and incompetence in allowing Cuban bloodhounds to be employed by the War Department in 1840 for ridding Florida of the Seminoles. Library of Congress

★ ★ ★

Cuban bloodhounds to remove Seminole Indians from their tribal lands in Florida. The use of the dogs particularly enraged abolitionists, who believed that the animals were really intended for hunting runaway slaves.

Van Buren's bloodhound brouhaha followed the first major economic crisis to dog an American president: the Panic of 1837, which was brought on mainly by land speculation associated with the opening of the West. The President was roundly criticized for resisting congressionally sponsored solutions while dining in the White House with silver knives and forks and plates of gold.

Leaders of the Whig Party saw the Panic of 1837 as an opportunity to oppose Van Buren and reassert the powers of Congress. They nominated the aged general William Henry Harrison, hero of the Battle of Tippecanoe during the War of 1812, to run against Van Buren in 1840. According to a Whig campaign lithograph, Harrison was the first presidential candidate to be accompanied by a dog out on the hustings as he greeted voters. The caption under the picture explains that his dog "repeats the welcome" extended by the general "with a cordial and significant shake of the tail." And it adds: "If the looker-on will only watch close enough, he can see the tail absolutely shake."

Dogs became an important symbol in the Harrison campaign.

HARRISON'S TAIL-WAGGING CAMPAIGN PAL

A Whig campaign print shows William Henry Harrison and his dog
greeting a wounded War of 1812 veteran outside his log cabin, which
has a coonskin tacked to the wall and two barrels of hard cider
resting on the ground below it. The American flag flying above
the cabin is inscribed with the 1840 Harrison-Tyler ticket.

Library of Congress

★ ★ ★

A cartoonist's portrayal of Harrison's anticipated election victory pictures a pack of Whig hounds chasing the fox Van Buren toward the White House steps, where Harrison stands guard with a pitchfork. The hounds are dressed in open-ended hard-cider barrels. A Democratic newspaperman had recommended that the sixty-seven-year-old candidate should be put out to pasture with "a barrel of hard cider and a pension of $2,000," so he could spend his last days sitting and sipping by the fire in a log cabin instead of running for president. The Whigs pounced on the remark, turning it to their candidate's advantage. They publicized Harrison as the "log cabin and hard cider candidate," an image that, along with his tail-wagging campaign dog, endeared him to voters.

Tragically, the victorious Harrison caught pneumonia while delivering his ninety-minute inaugural address, hatless, in a freezing rain. He died a month later. John Tyler seized the presidency, thus settling the then-unresolved constitutional question on the vice president's right to assume the office when it became prematurely vacant. But he quickly disappointed fellow Whigs when they discovered he was no ally in their effort to undo the vast powers of the presidency established by Andrew Jackson.

The bold and assertive new president, however, had a soft heart for animals. At his Sherwood Forest plantation in Charles

City, Virginia, Tyler and his wife, Julia, were reported to have been "surrounded by various dogs, horses, and birds, to which they became very attached." Their idyllic life on the plantation was described in a letter from Julia to Margaret, her city-bound sister: "The President is in a large armchair near me with his feet raised upon the railing. Once in a while a scream from all hands, dogs and servants, causes us to raise our eyes to see a full chase after a poor little hare."

In 1844, the year he vacated the White House, Tyler surprised Julia by ordering an Italian greyhound puppy for her from Naples. Le Beau, as the young racing dog was named, arrived in New York City, first spending several weeks with Julia's mother, who prided herself on her veterinary skills. Her mother claimed to have acquired those skills, "when all humans of my immediate acquaintance fell suddenly well."

Julia finally received the greyhound with an explicit set of instructions from her mother about the care and feeding of the rambunctious Le Beau. "I think a great deal of him," her mother added. "But I would not take such a pet for a gift." Julia wrote back: "Little Le Beau is perfectly well and hearty and has the most unfailing attention." She did admit, however, that the greyhound puppy was "very rough on furniture and rugs and required constant attention and discipline."

Tyler, likewise, was so rough in thwarting the programs of his own Whig Party that he was burned in effigy all around the country and caused every cabinet member except Secretary of State Daniel Webster to resign. A political cartoon of the day showed Tyler setting his hunting dogs on the Whig coons, which were trapped in the hickory tree of his idol Andrew Jackson. Democrat James K. Polk, who would soon succeed Tyler as president, is portrayed as a knife-wielding, buckskinned hunter, about to slice the tail off of Whig leader Henry Clay, shown as one of the coons.

Tyler lost any chance of being nominated to run again in 1844. But as presidential scholar Wilfred E. Brinkley pointed out, he nevertheless "prepared the way for the completion of the movement toward executive leadership started by Andrew Jackson."

FIDO IN AN INFORMAL POSE

*The Lincolns' pet dog looks forlorn, as if he understands that he's not
going to paw his way into the White House with the rest of the family.*

Meserve-Kunhardt Collection

★ ★ ★

CHAPTER FOUR

"ASSINATED LIKE
HIS MASTER"

ZACHARY TAYLOR TO
ABRAHAM LINCOLN

J AMES POLK WAS THE LAST PRESIDENT OF THE JACKSONIAN ERA, AND THE LAST WHOSE days in the White House were not consumed by the slavery controversy. Zachary Taylor, Millard Fillmore, Franklin Pierce, and James Buchanan all tried unsuccessfully to defuse the issue that threatened to destroy the union. Dogs were again employed in a whole flurry of political cartoons dealing with slavery.

Taylor was depicted in one such drawing as an indecisive, do-nothing leader who failed to endorse the Wilmot Proviso, which would have banned slavery in U.S. territories acquired during the Mexican War. Dressed in his old military garb, and accompanied by a bloodhound used for tracking down Seminole Indians and runaway slaves, the President is being asked: "Now then General, in one word, What er yer Principles? for d'ye see, if yer devoid o principle, yer aint fit to govern this great Nation, not by a darn'd long chalk." But it is not known whether Taylor, who died in office, ever owned a dog.

Neither is there any record of Fillmore, who finished Taylor's term, having a dog, although he was known to like them and to have chaired a series of meetings that led to the formation of the American Society for the Prevention of Cruelty to Animals. After leaving the White House, he became the ASPCA's vice president and contributed to the organization until his death in 1874.

Pierce and Buchanan, however, were both known for their dogs. In a lithograph picturing the street in front of Pierce's law office in Concord, New Hampshire, a dog can be seen barking at a passing team of oxen. But there is no indication that it was one of the seven miniature Oriental dogs that arrived with a large consignment of presents from Japan, marking the opening of diplomatic relations with the U.S. Besides the dogs, the gifts included plants, silks, swords, vases, parasols, and two birds. Pierce gave one of the Japanese dogs to Mrs. Jefferson Davis, whose husband would become president of the Confederacy. It was said she accepted the tiny animal "to the great annoyance of many who stepped on him."

Buchanan, who became so pessimistic about the resolution of the slavery question that he predicted he would be the last president of the United States, owned a huge Newfoundland named

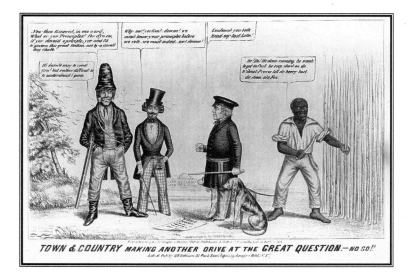

TOWN & COUNTRY MAKING ANOTHER DRIVE AT THE GREAT QUESTION.—NO GO!!

THE SLAVERY ISSUE DOGGED ZACH TAYLOR

Here President Zachary Taylor is flanked by two bloodhounds,
reminders of the hunting dogs used by his and Van Buren's
administrations to track down Seminole Indians and runaway slaves.
He is being confronted by a country bumpkin and an urban dandy
who question his principles. The unsigned Wilmot Proviso lies on the
ground at Taylor's feet. The slave cutting sugarcane behind the
President says: "He! He! He dam cunning. he wants to get in fust. he
keep dark on de Wilmot Provis till de beery last. de dam ole Fox."

Library of Congress

★ ★ ★

BUCHANAN'S BELOVED LARA

The first bachelor president's First Dog was a giant Newfoundland named Lara. This portrait of the dog appeared in Frank Leslie's Illustrated Weekly *at the time of Buchanan's inauguration. Before he became president, Buchanan served as the U.S. ambassador to Great Britain, where he was presented to Queen Victoria. While abroad, he exchanged weekly letters with his niece, Harriet Lane, asking her for a full report on Wheatland, his country estate in Pennsylvania. "How is Lara?" the future president wanted to know. "He sounded homesick," reported Harriet.* General Research Division, The New York Public Library: Astor, Lenox, and Tilden Foundations

★ ★ ★

Lara. The 170-pound dog romped the grounds of his Wheatland estate near Lancaster, Pennsylvania, before high-tailing it to Washington.

At the time of Buchanan's inauguration in 1857, *Frank Leslie's Illustrated News* ran a picture of the President's dog with the following description: "Prominent also [on his estate] is Mr. Buchanan's Newfoundland dog Lara; remarkable for his immense tail and his attachment to his master." The magazine further predicted: "This dog will hereafter become historical as a resident of the White House." Lara became a White House celebrity, known for his peculiar habit of lying motionless for hours with one eye open and one eye closed.

Newfoundlands, or Newfies as they are called, are so large and furry they have been mistaken for bears—not exactly the kind of pet a president might be expected to have bounding around the finely decorated rooms of the White House. It was especially unusual for Buchanan to have acquired a Newfie, since the breed had only been in existence for about fifty years. In fact, these dogs were almost wiped out when the governor of Newfoundland, in an effort to promote sheep raising, decreed a limit of one per household.

Perhaps it was Lord Byron's oft-quoted eulogy to his beloved Newfoundland, Boatswain, that decided Buchanan to seek out

FIDO AND HONEST ABE'S HOME

All the hoopla in Springfield, Illinois, attached to Lincoln's political campaigns frightened Fido, the family dog. Even his paw prints were sought as souvenirs by the future president's followers.

Library of Congress

★ ★ ★

one of these rare, oversized beasts. The English poet described Boatswain as: "One who possessed beauty without vanity, strength without insolence, courage without ferocity, and all the virtues of man without his vices."

While Lara was probably the biggest dog that had ever been given the run of the White House, one of the smallest also dwelled there during Buchanan's term. Because Buchanan was a bachelor, his niece, Harriet Lane, served as First Lady. She was the recipient of a tiny toy terrier named Punch, a gift from the U.S. consul in South Hampton, England, who described the dog as so small that "it might be put under a quart bowl." A writer who covered social and political life in Washington explained that "the little stranger was a nine-days' curiosity at the White House where it was exhibited to all who were on visiting terms with Miss Lane."

The first recorded photograph of a presidential dog came with the election of Abraham Lincoln. Fido, a yellowish-brown mongrel belonging to the Lincoln family, was taken to F. W. Ingmire's studio in Springfield, Illinois, just before Lincoln left for his inauguration in 1861. There, stretched out on a cloth-covered washstand, with his front paws propped up and with the tail he loved to chase stretched out behind him, the dog posed docilely for the portrait that would become a treasured family keepsake.

The picture now resides in the Illinois State Historical Library with other objects of Lincoln memorabilia.

Lincoln had sensed that Fido wouldn't be happy in Washington. He had already noticed how the clanging church bells and booming cannons announcing his nomination had scared the dog. And he had also seen how the steady stream of local politicians patting Fido's head at the time of his debates with Democratic candidate Stephen Douglas had forced the bewildered animal to take refuge under the family's horsehair sofa. So when Lincoln was elected president, he informed his sons, Tad and Willie, that Fido was going to stay behind in Springfield. He told the boys they would have to satisfy themselves with the newly taken portrait of their pet.

Mary Lincoln hated pets and was not unhappy to get rid of Fido. But her husband, who as a boy had rescued and raised an injured mutt named Honey, demanded that Fido be given special care. It was finally decided that he should stay with the Roll family, close friends of the Lincolns. Specific orders were given that Fido was never to be tied up or scolded for entering the house with muddy paws. Because he was used to being fed scraps, he was also to be allowed in the dining room at mealtimes. Finally, to make Fido feel more at home, the Rolls were even given the Lincolns' horsehair sofa.

THE LAST RAIL SPLIT BY "HONEST OLD ABE."

WATCHING HIS MASTER DIVIDE THE OPPOSITION

Fido and Tad watch Lincoln split the opposing Democrats in this 1860 cartoon. While Stephen Douglas was the official Democratic nominee, John C. Breckinridge of Kentucky became the standard-bearer of the Southern Democrats and John Bell of Tennessee, nominee of the National Constitutional Union. If these Southern Democrats hadn't defected, Douglas would have easily defeated the Illinois rail splitter, as Lincoln was known. Library of Congress

* * *

PRESIDENT LINCOLN'S DOG.

FIDO'S OFFICIAL PORTRAIT

Because Tad and Willie Lincoln's pet dog was left in Springfield, the boys were given this picture of Fido to take to Washington. It is said young Abe once found a mutt with a broken leg in the woods. He made a splint and took the animal to a cave to which he delivered food. Finally he brought the dog home, naming her Honey. Sometime later Abe was trapped in a cave. It was Honey who led the rescue party.

Meserve-Kunhardt Collection

Lincoln's victory, achieved with only 40 percent of the popular vote, had been greeted with ominous threats of secession throughout the South. There was some question, therefore, whether the family would ever see Fido again. Said the President-elect as he bid farewell to the citizens of Springfield, "I now leave not knowing when, or whether ever, I may return, with a task before me greater than that which rested upon Washington."

By the time of his inauguration, six Southern states had already seceded, and Lincoln's appeal for peaceful resolution of the slavery issue was quickly rejected by secessionist leaders. The bombardment of Fort Sumter on April 12, 1861, ignited the Civil War, though it wasn't until two years later that Lincoln issued his famous Emancipation Proclamation, freeing the slaves.

About that same time came news of Fido's well-being from the president's former barber, William Florville. "Tell Taddy that his Dog is a live and Kicking doing well," the barber wrote. But Tad had already acquired another dog. In fact, the President was reported to have rushed in one day and announced that Tad's dog had just given birth to "the prettiest pups you ever did see." And despite his military and political problems, Lincoln even took time out to help name them. It was also reported that the President spread the joyful news of the puppies' arrival to "every senator, cabinet member and foreign diplomat he met."

In 1864 Lincoln was reelected. This time the candidate, who had formerly been dismissed as a "prairie lawyer" and "back-woods president," obtained 55 percent of the popular vote and an overwhelming electoral college majority. Early in the campaign he claimed to have been resigned to defeat. But his abiding commitment to a free election, even in a time of war, won him great support. "If rebellion could force us to forgo or postpone a national election," he told a crowd celebrating his victory, "it might fairly claim to have already conquered and ruined us."

On April 14, 1865, with the Civil War won, Lincoln was shot by actor John Wilkes Booth; he died the next day.

The President's body was taken home by train to Springfield for burial. Fido was present. It was said that the dog forlornly watched the funeral procession that was followed by Old Bob, Lincoln's horse and Fido's four-legged pal.

Less than a year after the President's assassination, Fido strayed from the Rolls' house. "The dog in a playful manner put his dirty paws upon a drunken man sitting on the street curbing," wrote John Roll to the Lincoln family, which had returned to Washington. "In his drunken rage the man thrust a knife into the body of poor old Fido. So Fido, just a poor yellow dog was assinated [sic] like his illustrious master."

Fido, however, lives on not only because of the early glass plate photographic image made of him by F. W. Ingmire. He is also believed to be the inspiration for one of Honest Abe's favorite parables.

"If you were to call a tail a leg, how many legs would this dog have?" Lincoln once asked his sons. The boys, naturally, answered five. "No," replied the President. "Calling a tail a leg doesn't make it a leg."

WHITE HOUSE AND DOGHOUSE

Benjamin Harrison's collie, Dash, had a doghouse situated so as to

let him keep tabs on presidential comings and goings.

President Benjamin Harrison Home

* * *

CHAPTER FIVE

BOWWOWING
TO CONGRESS

ANDREW JOHNSON
TO WILLIAM MCKINLEY

THE ASSASSINATION OF LINCOLN AND THE SUDDEN SUCCESSION OF ANDREW JOHNSON began a thirty-year struggle between the White House and Congress, resulting in a serious erosion of presidential power. Drawings of dogs were still being relied on heavily in cartoons to satirize the problems faced by the eight presidents of the period. At the same time, the close companionship between dog and president became much more evident with the development of photography in the latter half of the nineteenth century.

During the two terms of the hard-drinking Ulysses Grant, a kennelful of dogs was pictured living—while many more were also mysteriously dying—in the White House. Son Jesse's memoir (*In the Days of My Father General Grant*) described his various dogs' strange inability to survive their lofty new status as presidential pets. "In the early days of my new home," he wrote,

AN AU-GUST CONVENTION.

MUZZLING ANDREW JOHNSON'S BACKERS

The National Union Convention, which met in Philadelphia in 1866 to create a party that would back President Andrew Johnson's Civil War reconstruction program, was portrayed in this cartoon as a collection of muzzled dogs, each labeled with the name of a state. The movement ultimately failed, and anti-Johnson Republicans achieved more than a two-thirds majority in both houses of Congress. Two years later the Republican Congress voted to impeach Johnson, but the Senate failed to convict him. Library of Congress

★ ★ ★

"the only sorrows I ever knew in the White House came to me. I possessed all the normal small boy's fondness for a dog and acquired several in rapid succession, only to have each, in turn, die. Over each demise my grief was bitter. Then someone presented me with a magnificent Newfoundland. When this dog came, father called the White House steward. He asked no questions, made no accusations.

" 'Jesse has a new dog,' he said simply. 'Ya may have noticed that his former pets have been peculiarly unfortunate. When this dog dies every employee in the White House will be at once discharged.' " But then Grant, ordinarily a mild-mannered man who disliked hunting and hated the sight of blood, was not known for his tact. As one historian wrote, "Despite a highly successful military career that suggested unusual executive ability, General Grant was unable to transfer his success from the battlefield to the White House."

Jesse Grant also wrote how Faithful, as he christened his big dog, "never had a press notice and was no better known than John Smith's dog." But Grant's son also made it clear that Faithful was not lacking in attention. "I never owned a more deserving dog," he wrote.

Another dog, an unpedigreed yellow-and-black bitch named Rosie, resided happily in the Grant White House. Rosie, unlike

the First Family's other dogs, was cared for by Albert the coachman, who came there with the Grants. Jesse Grant reported that
when Albert gave the president's horses, Cincinnatus and Egypt,
their daily lumps of sugar, Rosie kept eyeing the coachman wait-
ing for hers. Albert, Jesse mentioned incidentally, "was the most
thoroughly contented man I have ever known," and presumably
that included his father, the President, whose efforts to deal with
a disobedient Congress were being increasingly stymied.

President Rutherford B. Hayes, who slipped into the White
House with a margin of one electoral vote in 1876, and then only
after a compromise was worked out by Republican and Democratic leaders, made up for his slim victory with a full comple-
ment of dogs. He had a cocker spaniel named Dot, a small black
mutt named Jet, a Newfoundland called Hector, Grim the greyhound, Deke the English mastiff, hunting pups Juno and Shep,
plus a pair of shepherd dogs. Some of these dogs, however, were
acquired after he retired to his home in Spiegel Grove, Ohio, in
1880. Hayes wrote to one of his children that, along with the
Siamese cat, the goat, and the mockingbird, the many dogs gave
"a Robinson Crusoe touch to our mode of life."

The President's diary frequently mentioned his dogs as well as
the difficulties he experienced trying to housebreak congressional leaders of their habit of passing out patronage positions, a

"REB" AND "BILLY BUTTON" CARRYING THE PRESIDENT'S CHILDREN TO SCHOOL.—[Sketched by Theo. R. Davis.]

HEADING OUT FOR SCHOOL

One of the White House dogs follows along as President Grant's children are driven to school in a horse-drawn carriage. This picture appeared in Harper's Weekly, *a year after Grant's election.*

Library of Congress

★ ★ ★

YOUNG FAITHFUL

Jesse Grant, in his memoir about life with his famous father, claimed the only sorrows he knew living in the White House resulted from the mysterious deaths of several of his dogs. Library of Congress

* * *

task which, he reported, "exposed me to attack, misconstruction, and the actual hatred of powerful men."

His canine notations, for the most part, were much cheerier. "Yesterday," wrote Hayes, "we received by express a beautiful brindle, mouse-colored greyhound named Grim." The two-year-old dog was a gift from Mrs. William DuPont of Wilmington, and as the President added, "He is good-natured and neat in his habits . . . and took all our hearts at once." However, Hayes went on to explain, "Our other dogs soon discovered that their noses were out of joint. Hector, the Newfoundland, and Dot the terrier [actually a cocker spaniel], both about six months old, at first showed some jealousy of the stranger, but his social qualities and talents quickly established good relations with them."

Grim became an overnight national celebrity. When his life suddenly ended, the whole country voiced its sorrow in a deluge of condolence letters. "The death of Grim has made us all mourn," wrote Hayes. "He was killed instantly by a train at Pease's Crossing. He stood on the track evidently expecting the train to turn out for him. All [horse] teams turned out for him."

The struggle between the president and Congress continued under Republican James Garfield, who was called a Mugwump for doggedly refusing to support the party ticket. This factionalism, demonstrated by the thirty-six ballots that it took just to

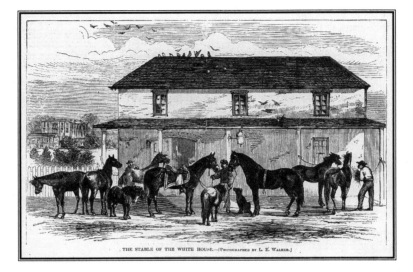

THE STABLE OF THE WHITE HOUSE.—[Photographed by L. E. Walker.]

ALBERT AND ROSIE

Albert, the Grant family's coachman, feeds lumps of sugar to the President's horses as dog Rosie looks on hopefully. The White House stable was built in 1864 at Lincoln's request. During Grant's two terms it was rigidly run by Albert, who, it is said, not only ate with the animals but talked to them as well. Library of Congress

★ ★ ★

"LEMONADE LUCY" WITH DOT

Cocker spaniel Dot tries to climb into the lap of Lucy Hayes, as the
President (standing) looks on. An active temperance advocate, she
was nicknamed Lemonade Lucy. Her many other pets included a cat
named Piccolomini, a peacock, and a mockingbird. Lucy loved all
animals, and according to the President's diary, they loved her, too,
and could hardly contain themselves when she returned home.

Rutherford B. Hayes Presidential Center, Fremont, Ohio

nominate him, further weakened his power. Nevertheless, Garfield continued Hayes's habit of vetoing bills willy-nilly and named his dog Veto to advertise his recalcitrancy. But this president had a silly sense of humor. Once when he was attending a White House reading by Charles Dickens of *A Christmas Carol*, a barking dog interrupted the English novelist. For months afterward, Garfield greeted anyone who had attended the reading by howling "Bow wow wow!"

Garfield finally seemed to be making headway with Congress, particularly on civil service reform, when a deranged lawyer named Charles Guiteau shot him in the back. The President lingered on for ten weeks before succumbing. His successor, former vice president Chester Arthur, who had once been removed as the collector of the Port of New York for flagrant political abuses, surprised everyone by signing into law a civil service reform act. However, he added to the mystery of his own life—and of his interest in dogs, if any—by burning all his personal papers and pictures the day before he died.

Although his successor, Democrat Grover Cleveland, was a hard-working president, he lost his bid for reelection in 1888 when the electoral college overrode the popular vote and picked Republican Benjamin Harrison. Then in 1892 Cleveland came out of retirement and was elected again, becoming the only

SECOND TERM

President Grover Cleveland stunned the nation in his first term when at forty-nine he married his twenty-one-year-old ward, Frances Folsom, in a spectacular White House wedding. Their son Richard, the family dog (whose name is not known), and the President pose as a happy threesome in front of the White House during Cleveland's second term. Library of Congress

★ ★ ★

president to serve two nonconsecutive terms. He tried hard to alter the principle of legislative supremacy, although between his two terms, Harrison had willingly bowed to Congress's desire for control.

These two presidents did have one thing in common: dogs. Several resided in the White House during both of their administrations. Cleveland's young wife Frances, the twenty-one-year-old ward whom he married in a glittering White House ceremony, turned out to be a lover of all kinds of animals. When this fact was publicized, a Milwaukee man sent her a nine-month-old Japanese poodle (some say it was a Pekingese), described as the smallest "pug dog" in the U.S. It weighed just a pound and a half. The newlyweds also owned what appears to have been a dalmatian.

Between Cleveland's two terms, Benjamin Harrison, the grandson of former president William Henry Harrison, placed a fancy doghouse right next to the White House to accommodate Dash, the handsome collie he obtained for his grandchildren. He gave them many other pets as well, including two opposums and a goat named Old Whiskers that was said to resemble the President because they both had pointed beards. One day while Harrison awaited his carriage on the North Portico, Old Whiskers bolted out through the White House gate pulling the three

FIRST DOG DASH
HAD A WHITE HOUSE OF HIS OWN

Benjamin Harrison's collie Dash had his private quarters next to the White House. The dog was a gift from the President to his grandchildren, who, along with their parents, all lived in the White House with a second dog named Jack and an assortment of other pets.

Library of Congress

★ ★ ★

JACK AND OLD WHISKERS, THE RUNAWAY GOAT

Russell Harrison, the President's son, and his daughter Marthena
pose with Jack at their feet. Sitting in the cart behind Old Whiskers
are two other grandchildren of the President, young Benjamin
Harrison McKee and his sister Mary McKee. This time Old Whiskers
behaved himself and didn't bolt while the picture was being snapped.

President Benjamin Harrison Home

* * *

MYSTERY DOG AND THE DOOMED MCKINLEY

An anonymous black dog foreshadowed McKinley's assassination while the President (second from right) was viewing Niagara Falls. This photograph was taken on a side trip from the Pan-American Exposition in Buffalo, where McKinley was later shot. The assassin admitted he had nothing against McKinley. He merely wanted to abolish the government, he said. Surprisingly, no other photographs are known to exist of McKinley with a dog. Even when he campaigned from his front porch in Canton, Ohio, proclaiming "a full dinner pail" for all, no dogs snuck into the picture. Library of Congress

★ ★ ★

young grandchildren in the cart behind him. The President took off in hot pursuit, holding on to his top hat with one hand and waving his cane with the other, with collie Dash dashing along at his heels.

Cleveland's turbulent second term, during which he was rebuked for using troops to intervene in the bloody Pullman strike against the railroads, was followed by a dramatic Republican victory in 1896 that catapulted Ohioan William McKinley into the White House. He was the last Civil War veteran to be elected president. Like Harrison, he brought with him a deep respect for congressional primacy. But as far as is known, he didn't bring any dogs.

Politically, he didn't need them. The Spanish-American War victory, which gave Puerto Rico and the Philippines to the U.S., greatly enhanced McKinley's stature as commander in chief and assured his reelection in 1900. But on September 6, 1901, while attending the Pan American Exposition in Buffalo, McKinley was shot by anarchist Leon Czolgosz. A few hours earlier the President had stood gazing serenely at Niagara Falls with an anonymous black dog seeming to haunt his steps. The dog has never been identified. But like a black cat, it was belatedly regarded by the press as having been a bad omen.

The identity of that anonymous black dog in the picture will probably forever remain a mystery. On the other hand, McKinley's legacy, as the president who extended U.S. territory to the Caribbean and to the Pacific, will always be remembered. His actions presaged the more dominant role chief executives would play in the twentieth century—a time, too, when the canine population of the White House increased by leaps and bounds.

A LITTLE LAP TIME AFTER THE HUNT

Whether he was out in the boondocks or in the White House, Skip always found President Theodore Roosevelt's lap a good place to snooze. Here at a Colorado hunting cabin, they both enjoy a little quiet time after tracking a bear. Theodore Roosevelt Collection, Harvard College Library

CHAPTER SIX

UNLEASHING THE
PROGRESSIVES

THEODORE ROOSEVELT
TO WOODROW WILSON

ANYTHING CAN HAPPEN NOW THAT THAT DAMN COWBOY IS IN THE WHITE HOUSE," complained Mark Hanna, chairman of the Republican Party, when McKinley was shot and forty-two-year-old Theodore Roosevelt became president—the youngest man ever to assume the office. Accompanied by his wife, Edith, six kids, and a full menagerie of dogs and other animals, Roosevelt charged into the presidential mansion like the Rough Rider he was during the Spanish-American War.

The high-spirited Roosevelt family, with all their pets, practically turned the White House (it was Roosevelt who gave the presidential mansion that name) into a zoo. Their canine contingent came with and without pedigrees and in assorted sizes, from Rollo, the enormous and good-natured St. Bernard, down to the diminutive Manchu, a black Pekingese presented to daughter Alice Roosevelt by the Empress Dowager Ci-Xi of China. Alice claimed she once spied Manchu dancing on her hind legs in the moonlight on the White House lawn.

The list of dogs seemed unending. There was Sailor Boy, the Chesapeake retriever who, if left behind, would swim after the presidential yacht. There was also Tip, Edith's mongrel, though she let it be known that any servant who denigrated the First Lady's dog by calling him a mutt would be fired. When Tip ran away, Edith went down to the dog pound to find a replacement. The new dog was promptly christened Mutt so the name-calling problem wouldn't arise again.

Son Kermit had a Manchester terrier named Blackjack, or Jack for short, who was forever being terrorized by the rowdy cat, Tom Quartz. When Jack died he was buried behind the White House. However, Edith couldn't bear to leave him there, as she said, "beneath the eyes of presidents who might care nothing for little black dogs." So at the end of Roosevelt's second term, in 1908, Jack's coffin was exhumed and finally laid to rest at Sagamore Hill, the Roosevelts' Long Island estate.

The bull terrier Pete was notorious. He nipped the leg of a naval officer, snapped at a few cabinet officers, and was finally banished to Sagamore Hill after ripping the pants of French ambassador Jules Jusserand.

The President's favorite, however, was Skip, a small, affection-

TR ROLLED OUT THE RED CARPET FOR ROLLO

This St. Bernard was the biggest of the family's dogs that roamed the White House during Teddy Roosevelt's two terms. As top dog he enjoyed special treatment from the President. TR, who loved animals and nature, used his presidential power to make sure that two of the country's greatest wilderness and wildlife areas — the Grand Canyon and Yosemite — were preserved for the American people to enjoy. He considered the Grand Canyon a beautiful hunting preserve and often shot bears there. Once when he refused to take aim at a mother bear because she was with a cub, newspapers headlined the story. Soon stuffed "Teddy" bears were selling like Cabbage Patch dolls have been for years. Theodore Roosevelt Collection, Harvard College Library

* * *

KERMIT WITH BLACKJACK, HIS BEDEVILED PAL

Blackjack, or Jack as he was called, was Kermit Roosevelt's dog. The terrier would have enjoyed White House life a lot more if he hadn't been taunted all the time by the family's playful cat, Tom Quartz, who chased him everywhere. Theodore Roosevelt Collection, Harvard College Library

★ ★ ★

ate dog of uncertain ancestry whom he picked up during a bear hunt in the Grand Canyon. Skip was probably a mongrel, though some canine experts now claim he was a rat terrier, an English breed that yips more than it barks and shows a strong inclination for hunting varmints. Roosevelt described Skip as a good fighter who would boldly stand his ground against a bear, just as he, himself, did against Congress while demanding the authority to direct the country's foreign policy, including building the controversial Panama Canal and mediating the Russo-Japanese War, for which he won the Nobel Prize. "Believers in a do-nothing policy," he wrote, "denounced me as having 'usurped authority'—which meant that when nobody else could or would exercise efficient authority, I exercised it."

Not always eloquent, Roosevelt nevertheless manipulated the press to achieve those ends, calling the presidency a "bully pulpit," and knowing how to use that pulpit to get things done. He became known as a "trust-buster" at home and an advocate of "dollar diplomacy" abroad. Reporters were attracted to his hard-charging, activist approach and referred to him affectionately as Teddy, or simply as TR, the first chief executive to be known by his initials.

But then this president loved to go after big game, both as politician and as hunter. The press was fascinated, following him

SKIP THE BEAR HUNTER—OR
WAS HE REALLY A RAT TERRIER?

Skip became the constant pal of the President, who admired his pluck.
Here Skip waits as TR tries to shoot a bear out of a tree. Skip's other
White House pal was young Archie Roosevelt's pony, Algonquin.
When Algonquin saw Skip coming, he would pretend to run away,
but would then slow down just enough to let the dog jump aboard
for a ride. Library of Congress

and his dog on hunting expeditions out West. Skip's short legs sometimes made it hard for him to keep pace with the riders, so Roosevelt would scoop the little dog up onto his saddle. In the White House, Skip was a constant source of entertainment for the rambunctious Roosevelt children, called "bunnies" by the President. Seven-year-old Archie would run races with him down the wide second-floor hall. Roosevelt wrote: "Archie spreads his legs, bends over and holds Skip between them. Then he says, 'On your mark, Skip, ready! go!' and shoves Skip back while he runs as hard as he possibly can to the other end of the hall, Skip scrambling wildly with his paws on the smooth floor."

After the children went to bed, Skip would go find the President, who was usually reading, and hop onto his lap for a snooze. Skip finally died in 1907, during Roosevelt's last year in office. He had "a happy little life," said the president.

William Howard Taft, who had served as Roosevelt's Secretary of War, was elected president in 1908. He was the heaviest president ever to serve, a 350-pounder, who brought not only a dog to the White House, but his own cow, Mooly Wooly, to assure himself of a steady supply of milk. But Mooly Wooly's production didn't satisfy the enormous appetite of this president, and she was soon replaced by Pauline Wayne, a handsome and more bountiful Holstein.

Taft also brought with him a surprisingly more passive view of presidential power than that of his predecessor. He harbored misgivings about interfering in the legislative process, a weakness in his leadership that touched off a congressional revolt between Roosevelt's trust-busting insurgents and the Old Guard Republicans. Taft tried to mediate between them, but ended up in the doghouse, so to speak. In 1910, for the first time in sixteen years, the Democrats took control of the House of Representatives.

The sight of Pauline the cow grazing on the White House lawn led to changes at that house, too. When Metropolitan Opera star Enrico Caruso came to sing for the Tafts, he realized that their daughter Helen yearned for a more cuddly pet than a milk cow. He presented her with a cute little dog—some said with a tenor's high-pitched bark—which she gratefully named Caruso.

Teddy Roosevelt's deep irritation with Taft's lack of leadership triggered a disastrous Republican split in the 1912 election. Roosevelt finally decided to run again for president as the third-party Progressive, or Bull Moose candidate. He outpolled Taft, but lost the election to Democrat Thomas Woodrow Wilson, the former president of Princeton University and governor of New Jersey.

Wilson brought many innovative ideas to Washington,

OF THE TAFT FAMILY'S TWO DOGS,
ONE HOWLED *LA TRAVIATA*

During this official portrait, the First Lady pats the head of the Taft's
old family dog, whose name unfortunately was not recorded for posterity,
while daughter Helen cuddles little Caruso. Library of Congress

WILSON'S MOUNTAIN BOY

Found among Woodrow Wilson's papers was this old pencil sketch he
made as a boy of the family greyhound, Mountain Boy. As an adult,
Wilson never wanted a dog bounding around the White House.
Woodrow Wilson House/National Trust, Washington, D.C.

★ ★ ★

announcing what he called his New Freedom Program. It resulted in creation of the Federal Reserve, which reformed the nation's banking system, as well as passage of the Federal Trade Commission Act and Clayton Antitrust Act, both designed to prevent unfair business competition.

He also brought sheep and a tobacco-chewing ram named Old Ike to graze in Pauline's place on the White House lawn. But unlike his immediate predecessors, he brought no dogs.

As a boy, Wilson, an aspiring young artist, had a greyhound called Mountain Boy, whom he liked to sketch. Mountain Boy obviously made a lasting impression. Wilson told his friends and political cohorts that dogs were instinctively good judges of human character. "If a dog will not come to you after he has looked you in the face," he claimed, "you ought to go home and examine your conscience."

As an intellectual and former professor, Wilson was given to examining his own conscience, and was often plagued by it. That's probably what kept him from plunging the U.S. into World War I at its outset. "He kept us out of war," became his 1916 reelection slogan, although the sinking of the ocean liner *Lusitania* and further acts of aggression by the Germans forced him to finally declare war the following year—"to make the world safe for democracy," he proclaimed. But his futile attempt

JUST CALL ME BRUCE

Whitestock Service Man, AKC 392,496 and aka Bruce, was given to President Wilson shortly before the President's death. The alert pup with upstanding ears and piercing eyes was a combination of Whitestock and Artesian bloodlines. Because of Wilson's failing health, the breeder said he purposely trained the dog for "companionship and house behavior."

★ ★ ★

to gain Senate ratification of the League of Nations, which he hoped would prevent future wars, so exhausted him that he suffered a stroke in 1919 from which he never recovered.

Wilson, however, did not go to the grave dogless. Shortly before he died, he was presented with a bull terrier. Named Whitestock Service Man, or Bruce for short, the handsome dog with piercing eyes and upstanding ears came from an admiring breeder. He complimented the President "for his wonderful gameness under suffering and adverse circumstances, and above all for his natural inherent love for his fellow man." In this note to the President, the breeder added, "I, with my little Scotch wife, could not conceive of a better gift, or a more appropriate one than a dog that showed the same characteristics."

FIRST FAMILY AND FIRST DOG

Laddie Boy frequently joined Warren and Florence Harding in
official White House photographs. The dog became such a celebrity
that critics claimed Harding was using the animal to compensate for
his own failings as president. Ohio Historical Society

★ ★ ★

CHAPTER SEVEN

IN THE DOGHOUSE
AT THE WHITE HOUSE

WARREN HARDING TO
HERBERT HOOVER

WARREN HARDING ONCE SAID, "I AM NOT FIT FOR THIS OFFICE AND SHOULD never have been here." And he probably was right. Yet his triumph by a huge majority in 1920 signified an end of the progressive era and a moratorium on reform. "Return to Normalcy" had been his Republican campaign theme. A handsome man who was devoted to his dogs, this president relied on canines to abet his campaign and later to help lead him out of a political morass.

The Hardings came to the White House with an English bulldog named Oh Boy. He was a sickly little creature and soon died. But his replacement, the airedale Laddie Boy—or Caswell Laddie Boy, his full pedigree name—became the President's constant companion and a White House celebrity.

Laddie Boy knew the President by his first name. First Lady

Florence Harding would hand the dog the morning newspaper and say, "Take this to Warren." Then with the rolled-up paper clenched in his teeth, the dog would trot off to find his master. Laddie Boy would also participate in the President's favorite pastime, happily retrieving his golf balls out on the White House lawn.

This animal, unlike all the presidential dogs before him, got involved in the workings of the government. Not only did he have his own hand-carved cabinet chair and sit in on high-level meetings, he was also often on the front steps of the White House to greet official delegations. Although he was so well known to reporters that they frequently quoted him in mock interviews, Laddie Boy failed to deflect attention from the excesses that soon engulfed the Harding administration—scandals and payoffs that were part of Harding's "Spoils System."

Once Harding even tried to use a fictitious correspondence between Laddie Boy and a vaudeville dog named Tiger to defend his loyalty to several presidential appointees who turned out to be defrauding the government. Published in a political magazine called *The National*, a letter from Tiger commended Laddie Boy for sticking by his master through thick and thin. Laddie Boy then replied that both man and dog could be undone by people who used friendship for their personal gain. Harding's airedale

"I HOPE SECRETARY DAVIS WILL GRANT ALL THE WATCHDOGS AN EIGHT-HOUR DAY."

GETTING THE LOWDOWN FROM LADDIE BOY

The Washington Star, *as is shown in this cartoon, conducted mock interviews with Harding's dog, supposedly getting his opinion on crucial canine issues. Even Congress took note of Laddie Boy. When it was about to kill the budget for the Marine band that played at presidential functions, one House member asked his colleagues which they preferred, "the President keeping his band music or listening to Laddie Boy racing around the White House grounds howling with a tomato can tied to his tail?" The band budget was approved.*

Library of Congress

* * *

BIRTHDAY BOY

On Laddie Boy's birthday, all the neighborhood dogs were invited to the White House for a party. Laddie Boy got first licks at the layer cake built of dog biscuits and smeared with icing. But then he was accustomed to special treatment, and even had his own servant, Willie Jackson, who stayed on through the Coolidge administration, when he assumed the formal title Master of the White House Hounds. Library of Congress

★ ★ ★

was thus echoing the anguish of his beleaguered master, who once remarked: "My God, this is a hell of a job! I can take care of my enemies all right. But my damn friends . . . they're the ones that keep me walking the floor nights."

Despondent and in poor health, the President and his wife took off in 1923 on a cross-country speaking tour ending in Alaska. He fell ill on the way home and died in San Francisco. Back in the White House, Laddie Boy was said to have sensed something was wrong and howled for three days just prior to the President's death.

To avoid the pain of being constantly reminded of her late husband, the First Lady gave Laddie Boy away to the Secret Service agent who had guarded them on the fateful trip to Alaska. Though Harding served barely two years and was one of the country's least successful chief executives, his death produced an outpouring of national grief. As a result, the Newsboys Association decided to present Mrs. Harding with a remembrance of the President's famous dog. Some nineteen thousand members each chipped in one penny to be melted down and cast into a statue of Laddie Boy. Unfortunately she, too, died before sculptor Bashka Paeff completed the piece, which now resides in the Smithsonian.

Calvin Coolidge, Harding's vice president, was an unlikely

heir to the increasingly public presidency. Called Silent Cal for his sparse speech, he also believed in maintaining a public silence about legislation. In any case, as one historian stated: "He raised inactivity to an art," though this seemed only to enhance his popularity as president.

Coolidge's and his wife Grace's popularity were bolstered by what could be called their dogged instinct for PR. Their two white collies, Prudence Prim and Rob Roy, and their airedale, Paul Pry, became national figures, especially on Easter when Grace dressed them up in bows and bonnets for the annual egg-rolling contest on the White House lawn. The First Lady also insisted on posing with Rob Roy for an official portrait by Howard Chandler Christy, which today hangs in the China Room of the White House. Wearing a red dress to contrast with the snow-white collie (the President wryly suggested that she wear a white dress and dye the dog red), she got the frisky Rob Roy to sit still for the artist by feeding him candy.

The Coolidges had many other dogs—a pair of chows named Blackberry and Tiny Tim, a brown collie named Ruby Rough, a bulldog called Boston Beans, Peter Pan the terrier, King Kole the police dog, Bessie the yellow collie, Palo Alto the bird dog, and Calamity Jane the sheepdog. Rob Roy and his canine pals were said to have kept the White House maids in a "state of terror," chasing them through the halls "like a burst of bullets."

Adding to the canine profusion and confusion was Grace Coolidge's penchant for changing their names. Rob Roy, for example, was originally named Oshkosh, after the Wisconsin kennel from whence he came. Paul Pry, who was a half-brother of Harding's Laddie Boy, was first christened Laddie Buck. But Pry seemed more appropriate because, as the First Lady said, "he had his nose in everybody's business."

By whatever name they were called, the dogs would come running when Grace Coolidge whistled. The President on the other hand, according to a White House servant, "had to whistle until he was blue in the face to get their attention." But when the President yelled "supper," the dogs would follow him to the dining room. White House guest Will Rogers, describing a dinner with the Coolidges, wrote: "Well, they was feeding the dogs so much that at one time it looked to me like the dogs was getting more than I was." The famous American humorist then added, "I come pretty near getting down on my all fours and barking to see if business wouldn't pick up with me."

The "Great Engineer," as Herbert Hoover was called, brought to the 1928 presidential campaign a tremendous reputation for his service as wartime food administrator under Wilson and as

IN THEIR EASTER BONNETS WITH THE RIBBONS ON IT
Prudence Prim, who later died in the White House, and the First Lady are
both dressed in their Easter finest for the annual White House egg-rolling
contest. The Coolidge dogs were a wild bunch inside the presidential
mansion, but they docilely submitted to wearing bonnets for the party.
Financier Andrew Mellon stands between the President and First Lady as
the festivities begin. UPI/Corbis-Bettmann

* * *

Secretary of Commerce under Harding and Coolidge. Yet his political handlers worried that this conservative Republican, who had never run for any office, appeared too stiff and austere to get elected. Their solution was to circulate thousands of autographed copies of a smiling Hoover holding up the paws of his police dog, King Tut, as if to suggest that candidate and canine alike were happily begging for voter support. It worked. They made dog meat of Democrat Al Smith (the popular vote was 21.4 million to 15 million), allowing the bureaucrat Hoover and the obedient Tut to move into the White House together. But in the end, each showed a devastating lack of adaptability to his new surroundings. The President proved ineffective in dealing with the dire economic circumstances that caught the prosperous country by surprise, while the police dog became over-protective of his master, practically suffering a nervous breakdown in the process.

As a dog fancier, Hoover enjoyed having a whole pack of the animals around him, though Tut remained his true companion. Also present in the Hoover White House were two fox terriers, Big Ben and Sonnie; Glen the Scotch collie; Yukon, the Eskimo dog; Eaglehurst Gilette, the setter; Pat, another police dog; and Weejie, the elkhound. Then there was Patrick, a huge, tawny, gray-brown Irish wolfhound, whose pedigree name was Cragwood Padraic.

HOOVER'S WINNING CAMPAIGN PICTURE

Wearing an uncharacteristic smile and holding up the paws of King Tut in the typical canine begging position, Herbert Hoover solicited voter support with autographed copies of this photograph. The police dog was acquired by the candidate in Belgium during his stint as European emergency food administrator during the First World War.

Library of Congress

MRS. HOOVER'S IRISH WOLFHOUND

Cragwood Padraic was presented to the First Lady after she moved
into the White House. The majestic animal is shown here with her
breeder, Mrs. Norwood Smith of Urbanna, Virginia, a former
classmate of the First Lady. Renamed Patrick by the Hoovers, the
dog was a great-great-grandson of Cragwood Darragh, the most
famous Irish wolfhound ever bred in the U.S.

★ ★ ★

Considered "the lord of dogs" by the *American Kennel Gazette*, the Irish wolfhound dates back to the days of the Roman Empire. Ever since then, these aristocratic hounds—used extensively in wolf-ridden Ireland—have been associated with emperors, kings, and other members of royal families. These are the majestic animals that George Washington tried unsuccessfully to track down through a contact in Ireland.

Patrick came to the White House as a gift from breeder Mrs. Norwood Browning Smith, a schoolmate of the First Lady. Considering the size of the dog and his need for open fields of muscle-stretching space, it's a wonder he could be kept confined on the grounds at 1600 Pennsylvania Avenue. Even the feeding troughs for these mighty animals stand two feet off the ground so they don't have to stoop to eat. Because of his size, strength, and swiftness, Mrs. Smith thought the wolfhound would make an ideal guard dog for the President and his wife.

But even after Patrick's arrival, King Tut continued as the White House guard dog. He patrolled the fences at night, sniffing constantly for intruders, while stopping at all the checkpoints. The White House security chief claimed he considered Tut "a sergeant, not merely a sentry." But apparently the dog took his duties too seriously and suffered under the strain of these nightly patrols.

His master, on the other hand, underestimated the seriousness of the country's economic plight and the government's need to respond. He hesitated to take the bold action of offering direct federal aid to cope with the hammer blows of the stock market crash and Great Depression. So in the end, both president and dog were unable to meet the changing demands of the White House. King Tut became morose, sulked, and lost weight, forcing the President to send him away to recuperate. Instead, the poor, puzzled police dog pined away and died.

Hoover, who had always fought to keep his personal life as well as his public policy negotiations screened from view, didn't release the news of King Tut's demise for several months. He told friends that he didn't want the country to grieve over a dog at a time when banks were failing, breadlines were forming, and unemployment was soaring. But the fact is this conservative Republican president was too private a person to build a close relationship with reporters—or, for that matter, with Congress. As historian Elmer Cornwell wrote: "No future president could hope to emerge from his White House ordeal unless he was prepared in talent and temperament to cope with and master the demands of an age of mass communications."

Standing for reelection in 1932—this time without King Tut

in the picture—incumbent Hoover carried only six states. Democrat Franklin Delano Roosevelt, who would soon prove to be a master communicator, a bold political innovator, and a lover of dogs as well—won in a landslide.

As FDR prepared to drive up Pennsylvania Avenue to be sworn in for a
third term, his Scottie Fala naturally expected to go along. But a Secret
Service agent snatched him from the limo and sent him scampering into the
White House, where he sulked for several days before running away. He
was found by a stranger in front of the Capitol Theater. The President
speculated that Fala was merely trying to see a newsreel of the inaugura-
tion he had missed. UPI/Corbis-Bettmann

* * *

NEW DEAL, NEW BREED

FRANKLIN ROOSEVELT

TO LYNDON JOHNSON

HEN DEMOCRAT FRANKLIN ROOSE-VELT WAS SWORN IN ON MARCH 4, 1933, a third of the U.S. workforce—some 15 million men and women—was unemployed. And in thirty-two states all of the banks were closed. "The day of enlightened leadership has come," announced the new president.

Sometimes it seemed there were as many new dogs in FDR's White House as there were programs in his New Deal. During the twelve years and one month of his presidency, eleven canines of various sizes, breeds, and temperaments romped the White House. There was Blaze, son Elliot's bull mastiff, who, when locked in the library one day, chewed up all the towels. Blaze's moment of greatest fame came when he bumped a homeward-bound soldier off a plane. In desperation Roosevelt finally said to Elliot, "There's room for you, son, or for your dog. Which will it be?" Soon both departed.

Daughter Anna's two red setters, Jack and Jill, didn't go up Capitol Hill to fetch a pail of water but were sent to live in the White House while she was being divorced. After remarrying, Anna added a retriever named Ensign to the President's ménage, who retrieved everything that wasn't nailed down. The grandchildren Sistie and Buzzie brought their pet bulldog, Pal, to live there, too. But with so much canine competition around, Pal cracked up and threw himself into an empty White House fountain in an apparent dogicide attempt.

Unpredictable behavior and bad manners seemed to be the mark of most of the Roosevelt dogs. Winks, a Llewellin setter from Warm Springs, Georgia, where FDR received his polio treatments, gobbled up eighteen bacon-and-egg breakfasts—"quick as a wink," it was said—one morning in the White House mess before being apprehended. "The only reason he didn't wash it down with coffee," claimed the President, "was because it hadn't been poured." Always high-spirited, Winks died of a broken neck after running headlong into the White House fence. He was buried with full honors in Maryland's Rosedale Dog Cemetery.

Meggie, Eleanor Roosevelt's Scotch terrier, chased the White House maids and once bit famous newshound Bess Furman on the nose. Major, the President's black-and-white German shepherd, was banished to the family's Hyde Park, New York, estate

WINKS'S BIG BACON-AND-EGG HEIST

A newspaper photographer set up this reenactment of setter Winks gobbling up the eighteen plates of bacon and eggs that had been laid out in advance for early-morning diners in the White House mess. UPI/Corbis-Bettmann

* * *

FEEDING FALA

Besides rolling over on his back, as he is doing here, the Scottie was trained by the President to shake hands, so he would be prepared to greet visiting dignitaries, and to stand at attention on his hind legs for the playing of "The Star Spangled Banner." *None of the White House servants were allowed to feed Fala when the President was there.* FDR Library

* * *

THE INCORRIGIBLE DUO

*Meggie, the First Lady's Scotch terrier, and Major, the President's police
dog, both made headlines by biting VIPs. White House maids had to use
their dust mops and brooms to fend off Major before he was finally banished to the Roosevelt estate in Hyde Park, New York, after biting a
passerby who stuck a hand through the White House fence to pet him.*

Associated Press Photo

★ ★ ★

after practically ripping the trousers off of British prime minister Ramsay MacDonald at a time when Germany, where this
breed originated, was braced for war with Britain. However,
FDR's Great Dane (confusingly called President) made amends
by giving the King and Queen of England a warm tail-wagging
reception on their visit to Washington.

Perhaps it was the outbreak of hostilities in Europe that made
Roosevelt want to get the White House on better war footing. In
any case, he decided, there should be fewer problem dogs under-
foot. First to go was the big, clumsy sheepdog, Tiny Tim. Even
so, FDR's favorite cousin, Margaret Suckley, thought the President still needed some canine companionship to relieve the ten-
sion from America's growing involvement in the war. In 1940 she
gave him Fala, the black Scottie that became his ever-present pal.

As things turned out, little Fala became the biggest White
House publicity hound of all time. He was photographed more
often and received more fan mail than many presidents. More
important, he seemed to thrive on all the attention, unlike so
many First Dogs that were spoiled or driven to distraction by
their fame.

Wherever the President went, Fala was sure to follow. Sitting
between Roosevelt's two feet, the little dog's eyes appeared to glow
with pride as he witnessed the signing of the Atlantic Charter

FALA FOREVER

Fala, who is buried beside FDR in the rose garden of the late President's Hyde Park estate, has been resurrected and seated next to his master—in bronze that is—at the Franklin Delano Roosevelt Memorial, erected at Washington's Tidal Basin. Senator Carl Levin suggested including the famous Scottie in order to portray FDR's human side. Sculptor Neil Estern agreed, adding a quizzical Fala to this model of the monument. Neil Estern/ The Franklin Delano Roosevelt Memorial Commission

* * *

aboard the cruiser *Augusta*. Secret Service agents guarding Roosevelt on trips nicknamed him the Informer because the frisky Scottie's presence was a sure sign that the commander in chief couldn't be far away.

At home in the White House, Fala attended press conferences, played in a pen outside the Oval Office window during working hours, and in the evening joined the President in the study, often with martinis sloshing overhead, if FDR happened to be entertaining. There was no reason why Fala should have been excluded from the cocktail hour. After all, his father's registered name was Peter the Reveller. Come 7 P.M. FDR would feed Fala himself, making the Scottie perform his repertoire of tricks —rolling over, shaking hands, and begging—before allowing him to eat. At night Fala slept on a blanket next to the President's bed.

One of the few times Fala got the boot was when he jumped into the presidential limousine expecting to ride as usual with his master up Pennsylvania Avenue en route to FDR's third inauguration. "Not this time, Old Man," said the President sympathetically. And Fala didn't make the summit meeting with Stalin in Yalta either. But that took place shortly before FDR's death, when the ailing President appeared dog-tired.

A grieving Fala did ride right beside the First Lady in the

FELLER, WHO WAS NOT FOREVER

This bewildered cocker spaniel puppy, a gift from a woman in Missouri, arrived unannounced at the Truman White House shortly before Christmas in 1947. The little dog, which came in a crate simply marked FELLER, *made big news when the President gave him away to White House physician Brigadier General Wallace Graham. Irate dog lovers around the country accused the president of being anticanine.* UPI/Corbis-Bettmann

* * *

Bob Hannegan, Truman's postmaster general, gave this young Irish setter to First Daughter Margaret. She named him Mike. "What else could you name a dog given by a man named Hannegan?" she said. One evening, while chasing Mike around the South Portico, she noticed a brightly lit room with maps plastered over the walls. The President cautioned his daughter to keep quiet about her discovery of the top secret war room. Mike developed rickets from candy fed to him by the White House guards. After being cured, he was sent to live on a farm in Virginia. UPI/Corbis-Bettmann

* * *

THE GENERAL AND HIS SCOTTIES

While he was the Supreme Commander of Allied Forces in North Africa, Eisenhower kept company with two Scotties, Caacie, standing at attention much to the General's amusement, and Telek, looking on.

Dwight D. Eisenhower Library

★ ★ ★

HEIDI WASN'T WHITE HOUSE—BROKEN

President Eisenhower stopped smiling when weimaraner Heidi left a big yellow stain on the carpet in the Diplomatic Room of the White House. The nervous pet also showed a proclivity for jumping up in front of Mamie Eisenhower when press photographers tried to snap the First Lady's picture. Eventually Heidi was sent back to the Eisenhower's farm in Gettysburg, where no canine protocol had to be observed. Dwight D. Eisenhower Library

★ ★ ★

President's funeral cortege. And when Fala finally died, he was buried next to his master in the rose garden of Roosevelt's Hyde Park estate.

On April 12, 1945, the day FDR died, Vice President Harry Truman had been enjoying his afternoon bourbon-and-water with House Speaker Sam Rayburn when he was summoned to the executive mansion. Upon his arrival Eleanor Roosevelt put her arms around his shoulders and said softly, "Harry, the President is dead."

"Is there anything I can do for you?" Truman asked.

"Is there anything we can do for you?" she replied. "For you're the one in trouble now."

With the country still at war, it seemed incomprehensible that this "little man from Missouri," as some people disdainfully called him, could take Roosevelt's place. Yet Truman proved to be a stubborn and resolute leader, deciding in August to drop the two atomic bombs that quickly caused Japan to surrender, and then in 1950 committing American troops to combat in Korea. On the home front he introduced the Fair Deal to replace Roosevelt's New Deal, thus continuing his predecessor's ideas of a welfare state.

Yet, when it came to having dogs in the White House, Truman

JFK'S EARLY PREDILECTION FOR PUPS

While touring Europe during a summer vacation from Harvard,
twenty-year-old Jack Kennedy picked up this stray dog in the
Netherlands, which he named Dunker. The picture was taken during
a stopover in The Hague by Kennedy's traveling companion Lem
Billings. Eventually they gave up Dunker because he was too much
trouble and quarantine regulations would make it difficult to take
the dog out of the country. John F. Kennedy Library

★ ★ ★

Or so it seemed when the Kennedys took their personal K-9 corps on vaca-
tion. Caroline leans on Irish spaniel Shannon while playing with her
Welsh terrier Charlie. John John pets Pushinka's pups. Jackie reaches out
to Clipper. John F. Kennedy Library

* * *

JACKIE AND CLIPPER

German shepherd Clipper was given to Jackie by her father-in-law
Joe Kennedy to provide added protection around the White House.
Unfortunately there was considerable jealousy among the family's
canine collection. White House dog keeper Traphes Bryant claimed
"Clipper was jealous of Shannon, Charlie was jealous of Wolf, and
Pushinka was jealous of everybody." John F. Kennedy Library

* * *

might just as well have said, "The pup stops here." He didn't want them around.

He proved that early on when a woman from his home state of Missouri sent him a cute cocker spaniel puppy named Feller— not Fala. She thought that Truman, like Roosevelt, should have some canine companionship to ease the pressures of the job. Truman, however, proceeded to anger dog lovers throughout the country by giving little Feller away.

Eventually this president, who was nicknamed "Give 'em Hell Harry," relented and allowed his daughter Margaret to accept an Irish setter puppy as a present from Postmaster General Robert Hannegan. But Mike, as Margaret named her frisky new friend, had trouble outgrowing his puppyhood. He was also fed so much candy by the White House guards that he soon developed rickets. He was given away to a farmer in Virginia before the Trumans left the White House.

Dwight Eisenhower was a different story. Not only was he a Republican, but he was a dog lover right from his boyhood days in Abilene, Kansas.

During the hard-fought World War II North African campaign, a pair of Scotties had been at Ike's side. The one named Telek, it was widely whispered around headquarters, was a gift from the general's army driver and mistress, Kay Summersby. By

OVAL PLAYPEN FOR HIM AND HER

Lyndon Johnson peruses incoming telexes while his famous beagles, Him and Her, find the Oval Office a great place to play. The President gave his dogs the run of the White House and carried doggie treats for them in his coat pocket. During the violent Vietnam War protests when students were chanting, "Hey, hey, LBJ, how many kids have you killed today," he frequently summoned the dogs because, as he said, "They like me." Yoichi R. Okamoto, LBJ Library Collection

★ ★ ★

A BASKET FULL OF BEAGLES

LBJ loved puppies, and he also doted on movie czar Jack Valenti's
young daughter, Courtney, who is enjoying the basket crowded with Him's
grandpups. Blanco is looking on jealously. Yoichi R. Okamoto,
LBJ Library Collection

* * *

the time Ike and his wife, Mamie, moved into the White House, Telek had been replaced by another Scottie, Spunky, and Ike himself was being kept on a tighter leash by Mamie.

The Eisenhowers also arrived in Washington with a weimaraner named Heidi, who for some reason resented the First Lady being photographed. Every time a press photographer took aim at Mamie, Heidi would jump up protectively in front of her. Or perhaps the high-strung dog just wanted to get in the picture. In any case, Heidi's weak bladder finally resulted in her being called on the carpet by the President—the one she kept wetting in the Diplomatic Room—and being sent back to the farm in Gettysburg, Pennsylvania, where it didn't matter if she wasn't White House–broken.

As a military man, Ike was inclined to call disobedient politicians on the carpet for their lapses, too. When Arkansas Governor Orval Faubus defied the Supreme Court by refusing to let nine black students enter Central High School in Little Rock, Eisenhower gave him a dressing down and finally sent paratroopers to Little Rock to make his reprimand stick. And when the notorious Red-baiting senator Joseph McCarthy charged that Communists were undermining Ike's administration, the President made sure he was censured by the Senate. Ike preferred to leave matters like that to the men and women on Capitol Hill. His two-term

COMBINING BUSINESS AND SWIMMING

During a cooling dip with Yuki and grandson Patrick Lyndon
Nugent in the ranch pool, the President pauses to read a communiqué
from the White House. LBJ complained that Yuki was constantly
shedding silky white hairs on his clothes, but he kept on playing with
him anyway. First Lady Lady Bird Johnson finally got fed up with
her husband's infatuation with this dog. When the President tried to
include Yuki in the family portrait taken at Luci's wedding, she laid
down the law: "That dog is not going in the wedding picture!"

Yoichi R. Okamoto, LBJ Library Collection

* * *

YUKI AND LBJ'S HARMONIOUS RELATIONSHIP
Ambassador to the United Kingdom David K. E. Bruce looks on as the President and Yuki sing a duet in the Oval Office. Luci discovered the stray mutt wandering around a Texas gas station one Thanksgiving day. Her father quickly adopted the dog for his own, to make up for the loss of Him and Her, both of whom had died prematurely. Yuki survived his rigorous White House days and retired with Johnson to the ranch in Texas after the president decided not to run for reelection in 1968. Five years later, when the President died, the loyal Yuki was at his side. Yoichi R. Okamoto, LBJ Library Collection

* * *

Republican reign was therefore referred to as the "hidden hand" presidency.

Activist John F. Kennedy, at forty-three the youngest man ever elected president, called for a "New Frontier" and promised to "get this country moving again." The combination of a sluggish economy, simmering civil rights problems, and the intensification of the Cold War had returned the White House to the Democrats in 1960. And along with Jack, Jacqueline, Caroline, and later on, little "John John" Kennedy came the largest pack of dogs since Rough Rider Teddy Roosevelt lived there. That wasn't surprising, given JFK's puppy love, which dated back to his Harvard days when he couldn't resist picking up a cute Dutch mutt he found on a street in the Netherlands.

At the White House, Charlie, young Caroline's Welsh terrier, was "boss dog." He swam with the President in the pool and growled threateningly if another dog tried to push ahead of him at dinner time. But then Charlie was uncouth in other ways. He would sometimes lift a leg and pee on those who ignored him, or playfully bite the bottom of a gardener bending over to weed one of the White House flower beds.

There was also Wolf, a monster Irish wolfhound, sent to the First Family by a priest in Dublin who was also named Kennedy; Clipper, a German shepherd, a gift from the President's father;

Shannon, an Irish cocker spaniel presented by Prime Minister Eamonn deValera of Ireland; and of course Pushinka (meaning "fluffy" in Russian), the mutt that Soviet premier Nikita Khrushchev gave Caroline in the hope of reducing tensions with the U.S. following the 1962 Cuban missile crisis. It wasn't long before the highly publicized White House romance between Charlie and Pushinka added to the canine headcount, as well as the cacophany, with the arrival of puppies Butterfly, White Tips, Blackie, and Streaker.

During Kennedy's abbreviated term, television became a key element in the exercise of presidential power. His adept and well-timed TV appearances, sometimes with a dog or two in the picture, made a lasting impression on the American people. After more than thirty years, none of his successors have been able to match the winsome personality and quick wit displayed in JFK's televised press conferences.

Texan Lyndon Johnson's style of leadership was entirely different. Quickly grasping the reins of power after Kennedy's assassination on November 22, 1963, he rammed through Congress much of JFK's unfinished New Frontier agenda. But he credited most of those accomplishments to his own Great Society program. The Civil Rights Act of 1964 empowered the government to reduce racial discrimination. Other new laws provided for

Medicaid and air pollution control and expanded the government by creating a Department of Transportation as well as a Department of Housing and Urban Development. Even the White House doghouse was redesigned and enlarged under Johnson's personal supervision into what was described by the press as a "canine palace."

Like most ranchers, LBJ loved dogs. Beagles were his favorites. As Senate Majority Leader, his pal was a four-legged LBJ—Little Beagle Johnson. After all, Johnson's wife, Lady Bird, and his daughters Lynda Bird and Luci Baines were all LBJs, so why shouldn't the beagle be an LBJ too? ("It's cheaper if we all have the same monogram," Johnson once said.) When the dog LBJ died, his ashes were stored on top of the refrigerator until the cook insisted they be sent to Texas and buried at the ranch.

Johnson moved into the White House with two new beagles, Him and Her. The pair achieved instant celebrity status—even appearing on the cover of *Life* magazine—when the President picked them up by their long floppy ears. Although that episode got a mere yelp out of Him and Her, it brought howls of protest from horrified dog lovers throughout the nation. But all the screaming didn't alter the antics of this President and his pet beagles.

He swam with them in the White House pool, let them chase

each other in and out of the Oval Office, rode them around Washington in the backseat of his bulletproof limo, flew them to Camp David aboard his helicopter, fed them candy-coated vitamin pills, and included them in receptions for visiting chiefs of state—even after Him left a puddle in a chair during a tea party. And when Him fathered a litter of five, named Freckles, Kim, Little Chap, Dumpling, and Crasher, the President exclaimed that he just loved the "basket full of fresh, wiggly puppies."

Both Him and Her met untimely deaths and were replaced by another beagle named Edgar, given to the President by FBI director J. Edgar Hoover, who was always eager to curry favor with the White House.

There was also the neurotic white collie, Blanco, who bit Edgar's nose so badly the wound required several stitches. In another jealous outburst, Blanco urinated on a sculpture by Alexander Calder that was on loan from the Museum of Modern Art in New York City.

It was a stray mutt picked up in a Texas gas station by daughter Luci that stole LBJ's heart. Named Yuki, the little dog "spoke with a Texas accent," or so the president claimed. Johnson took Yuki everywhere. Like Harding's Laddie Boy, he attended cabinet meetings (but under the table, as a nonparticipant) and was present in the East Room for the signing of the Wholesome Meat

Act. Once, at a gathering of his top generals, Johnson shook Yuki's paw before shaking their hands, as if to let the military men know where they ranked. For the annual White House Christmas tree lighting ceremony, the President had Yuki dressed in a Santa suit, and even danced with the dog at Lynda Bird's wedding.

Best of all, Johnson liked to sing duets with Yuki for the benefit of Oval Office visitors. Holding the dog aloft over his own tilted-back head, the two would howl a happy tune together. Yuki retired to Texas with Johnson and was with him at the ranch in 1973 when LBJ died of a heart attack.

REFRESHING SUMMER DIP

Not being able to discard her fur coat, Liberty found the White House
fountains great for cooling off during Washington's scorching summers.
Her master, Gerald Ford, was a more serious swimmer, doing daily laps in
the indoor White House pool, which FDR had built and Ford had
refurbished. The athletic President didn't let the rigors of the Oval Office
stop him from keeping physically fit. Courtesy Gerald R. Ford Library

* * *

CHAPTER NINE

A DOGHOUSE DIVIDED

RICHARD NIXON

TO GEORGE BUSH

R EPUBLICAN RICHARD NIXON BECAME THE
FIRST PRESIDENT SINCE ZACHARY TAYLOR
to win control of the White House with a minority
of his party in both the House and Senate. The
Democratic Party had been deeply divided by the Vietnam War,
but it still controlled Congress. That didn't stop Nixon, who
opposed the welfare state, from trying to use the Oval Office as a
lever for his conservative policies. He also demonstrated conservative taste in his choice of dogs. Checkers, the charismatic cocker
spaniel who had helped rescue Nixon's political career and who
had been a playmate of his daughters, Julie and Tricia, while he
was vice president, was only a memory by 1969, and rumors that
plans were afoot to exhume Checkers from a pet cemetery in
New York and rebury him near his master on the Nixon Library
grounds in California proved false.

A French poodle named Vicky and a Yorkshire terrier named

NIXON'S CANINE CHRISTMAS

To celebrate Nixon's first Christmas as president, White House dog keeper Traphes Bryant posed this picture of Pasha (left), Vicky, and King Timahoe, with their own toy Santa, a miniature tree, and stockings filled with doggie toys and treats. National Archives

★ ★ ★

TOP DOG AND TOP ADVISER

Nixon chats with Secretary of State Henry Kissinger while Vicky sacks out on the Oval Office carpet. The President kept a supply of dog biscuits in his desk drawer in case any of the three White House dogs got hungry and obstreperous during one of these high-level strategy sessions. National Archives

* * *

Pasha were the children's pets when the Nixons moved into the White House. They were well-behaved animals, models of "dogcorum," you could say. And so was King Timahoe, the regally named Irish setter given to the President by his staff. Timahoe soon became famous for greeting visitors with a polite pawshake.

The President himself seemed no more comfortable around these canine members of his family than he did with anyone else. He would get tangled up in their leashes, and worried that a White House press photographer might snap his picture in an awkward pose with the dogs. He rarely appeared with them in public. In the end, Vicky, Pasha, and Timahoe were victims of the Watergate scandal, too, although *their* behavior was unimpeachable. Like Nixon, they were forced to give up their luxurious White House digs after the House Judiciary Committee voted to impeach their master. It seemed a foregone conclusion that Nixon would be tried and convicted by the Senate. He resigned instead, then shepherded his wife, daughters, and dogs onto Air Force One and flew home to California, leaving the White House to the dogless Vice President, Gerald Ford.

Ford had never run for national or even statewide office when he replaced Nixon on August 9, 1974. Nevertheless, he wisely proclaimed "healing the nation's wounds" as his primary objective

OVAL OFFICE GIRLFRIEND

When President Ford's photographer and confidant, David Kennerly, walked into the Oval Office with the surprise gift of a six-month-old female golden retriever, Ford couldn't resist getting down on his hands and knees to play with the pup. As a grown-up dog, Liberty followed Ford everywhere. Courtesy Gerald R. Ford Library

* * *

as president. First, he granted amnesty to the fifty thousand Vietnam War draft dodgers, and then pardoned Nixon to avoid the divisive spectacle of the disgraced leader standing trial.

Ford also tried to restore the media's respect by eliminating some of the trappings of Nixon's so-called "imperial presidency." He cut the White House staff by 10 percent and started referring to the White House as the "residency." He also instructed the Marine band to substitute the University of Michigan (his alma mater) fight song for "Hail to the Chief." And when it came to naming the female golden retriever puppy that was given to him as a surprise soon after he became president, he shied away from anything as regal sounding as King Timahoe. He finally settled on Liberty, a name that conveyed his own patriotic spirit.

Ford always had been partial to golden retrievers. As a congressman he owned a golden named Brown Sugar, but it died before he was appointed vice president. When he moved into the White House, his close friend and official photographer David Hume Kennerly decided Ford badly needed another dog to compensate for the loneliness of the job. Kennerly quickly located a breeder of champion goldens in Minneapolis and called him.

"Who's it for?" asked the breeder.

"That's a secret," said Kennerly.

PROUD MOTHER OF EIGHT

First Lady Betty Ford and daughter Susan join the president

in congratulating Liberty on a job well done.

Courtesy Gerald R. Ford Library

★ ★ ★

AMY'S GRITS

Amy leads the mutt she was given by her schoolteacher down the White House steps. Named Grits, the dog didn't get along with Amy's Siamese cat Misty Malarky Ying Yang. Courtesy Jimmy Carter Library

* * *

"We have to know if the dog's going to have a good home," the breeder insisted.

"Well, the couple's middle-aged. They live in a white house with a big yard and fence around it," explained Kennerly.

"Do they own or rent?" asked the breeder.

"I guess you could say they live in public housing," replied Kennerly, finally realizing he would have to stop the charade and tell the breeder whom the dog was for.

Liberty quickly became an Oval Office fixture, often reclining right next to the President's desk when she wasn't taking care of visitors who had overstayed their leave. A lot of the time the President walked Liberty himself. Early one morning he was awakened by a wet kiss, indicating that the dog needed to go out. Ford put on his bathrobe and slippers and took Liberty down in the elevator. But on their return, the elevator wouldn't work, and all the stairway doors were locked for security. Ford pounded on the walls, accompanied by Liberty's barking. A covey of Secret Service agents came running.

It was a joyous day in the Ford White House when Liberty gave birth to eight pups. In fact, the whole country seemed to celebrate. Pictures of the mother were in such demand that a rubber stamp of her paw print was made to autograph them with.

Unfortunately, Ford's popularity suffered from the "full, free

LUCKY WAS NO LAP DOG

Reagan's Bouvier des Flandres pup grew so big he was hard to handle. Here he is sharing his master's seat aboard the President's helicopter. Courtesy Ronald Reagan Library

★ ★ ★

and absolute pardon" given to Nixon. As president he was unable to summon sufficient public support to bring the aggressive and hostile Democratic Congress to heel. The television show *Saturday Night Live* had fun lampooning him as a head-bumping, foot-tripping bumbler (though as a former football star he was one of our most athletic presidents) with a stuffed dog that he would order to sit or heel. After casting sixty-six vetoes, most of them to block spending bills, Ford was narrowly defeated by Jimmy Carter in the 1976 election.

As a boy in Georgia, Carter owned a mutt named Bozo. But when he and his family entered the White House, they came with a cat named Misty Malarky Ying Yang, and no dog. That situation was quickly corrected by young Amy Carter's public schoolteacher, who presented her with a mongrel puppy that Amy named Grits.

Grits's celebrity was brief. During Heartworm Awareness Week he reluctantly let himself be dragged out in front of the White House for a televised blood test. But he tore off his muzzle and, showing his true grit, refused to let the veterinarian stick a needle into one of his veins. He also refused to be housebroken, leaving his mark on several White House carpets, thus sealing his fate as First Dog. Amy finally returned the recalcitrant mutt to her teacher.

THREE-POINT LANDING

Nancy, and Ronald are greeted by Rex Reagan on the White House lawn as they alight from the president's helicopter. The Cavalier King Charles spaniel lived up to his name (Rex means "King"), enjoying a lavishly appointed white Colonial doghouse with fancy red curtains before flying off to California at the end of Reagan's second term. Courtesy Ronald Reagan Library

Carter's success as president was just as spotty. He seemed to be trying to outdo Ford in eliminating the imperial trappings of the presidency. During the inaugural parade, for example, Jimmy and Rosalynn Carter stepped out of their limo and walked from the Capitol to the White House. On trips to the hinterland Carter carried his own suitcase. "Most people prefer a little pomp in their presidents," cracked House Speaker Tip O'Neill. Carter's diplomatic triumph in getting Egyptian president Anwar Sadat and Israeli prime minister Menachim Begin to sign the Camp David Accords was overshadowed by his inability to free the American hostages in Iran. Short on both style and accomplishments—not to mention White House dogs—Carter became the first president since Herbert Hoover to be denied a second term.

Ronald Reagan, though outspokenly conservative, restored the preeminence of the presidency with his stylish manner and speeches. He paid homage to FDR but challenged the ideas of the New Deal. "Government is not the solution of our problem," he proclaimed in his inaugural address. "Government *is* the problem." And although Reagan barely survived an assassination attempt in his first term and became tarred by the Iran-contra scandal in his second term, he emerged as the most popular president since Roosevelt.

MILLIE AND HER CHILDREN

*Although she enjoyed only one term in the White House, Millie's days
there were very productive. Here she proudly shows off five of her six
children to the President. Millie was a perfectly behaved First Dog. But
that was to be expected after the year she spent prepping for the job at the
U.S. Naval Observatory, the official residence of the vice president.
She died in 1997 at the age of twelve.*

Bush Presidential Library

* * *

Reagan, like Carter, arrived in Washington with nary a dog in sight. Finally, in 1985, at the start of his second term, a nine-week-old Bouvier des Flandres pup named Lucky joined the First Family. White House chief of staff Donald Regan described how young "Lucky dropped by my office for a doughnut every morning before galloping thunderously back to the residence."

But the cute pup grew to be two feet tall and eighty pounds heavy, becoming quite difficult for Nancy Reagan to handle. Hanging on to Lucky's leash for dear life, the petite First Lady would almost take off in flight. The big dog was enrolled in obedience school in the hope that five weeks of strict training would make him more manageable. But size, not behavior, was the problem, and Lucky, alas, proved to be unlucky and was packed off to the Reagan ranch in Santa Barbara, where he could romp freely.

His replacement was a Cavalier King Charles spaniel named Rex, who soon found himself ensconced in a private dwelling more ornate than that of any First Dog before him. A white clapboard doghouse with red window draperies and framed pictures of the President and First Lady on the wall was erected for Rex. It was designed by interior decorator Theo Hayes, the great-great-grandson of President Rutherford Hayes, who had filled the White House with dogs a hundred years earlier.

Rex went west with the Reagans, making way for springer spaniel Millie, who moved into the White House with "Bar" and the "Prez," as she called Barbara and George Bush in her "dogobiography," *Millie's Book*. The book jacket claims Millie dictated the 141 pages of text and picture captions to the First Lady. Perhaps the First Lady took a cue from the Prez's acceptance speech at the 1988 Republican convention, when he said, "Read my lips," and that's how the book came to be. As president, however, Bush abandoned his pledge of "no new taxes" while devoting most of his attention to foreign policy, particularly the Persian Gulf War. His neglect of the economy cost him a second term, and forced Millie to vacate her happy home at the First Doghouse earlier than anticipated.

But while she was still luxuriating at 1600 Pennsylvania Avenue, this articulate springer spaniel had some interesting things to say about her happy days there.

"I often sit in on the morning briefings," she wrote. But, tiring of what she called her "heavily scheduled life," she also admitted, "I sometimes want to go out and hunt for squirrels." Obviously, Millie found other targets of opportunity on the White House lawn. "So far the score is eight known kills," she bragged. "Four squirrels, three rats, and to Bar's great sorrow, a pigeon."

Millie also described how during a "movie night" at the White

House she gave birth to five daughters and one son. "I sat up, took a few deep breaths," she explained, "and had my first daughter. Bar called the Prez at the theater and told him that a babe had come. About every fifteen minutes a new pup arrived. At one time I heard George . . . whoops . . . the President ask her what they were, and Bar told him they all looked alike. To think that Bar thought she was going to help me when she couldn't tell a boy from a girl!"

Before leaving the White House, Millie worried that her own popularity might be overshadowing the President's. "I overheard the Bushes talking the other night," she confessed near the end of her saga. "Some discussion about me keeping a lower profile."

Well, once Millie became a pedigreed author that was impossible. *Millie's Book* soared to the top of the bestseller lists.

SOCKS'S HIGH POSITION

Ignoring his need for a First Dog, President Clinton wound up a morning jog with First Cat Socks perched on his shoulder. The Clintons reportedly flirted a few times with the idea of getting a golden retriever before falling in love with Buddy, a chocolate Labrador retriever.

Agence France Presse/Corbis-Bettmann

* * *

CHAPTER TEN

WEAPONS OF MASS DISTRACTION

BILL CLINTON, GEORGE W. BUSH, AND BARACK OBAMA

ECAUSE LIFE-AND-DEATH DECISIONS ARE MADE EVERY DAY IN THE OVAL OFFICE, IT'S been called the loneliest place in the world. A number of presidents have endured it without a dog to keep them company. But would history have been different with a little canine intervention? Possibly so.

During the financial crisis resulting in the Panic of 1837, for example, might the presence of an affectionate dog have helped bachelor Martin Van Buren survive the beating he took from Congress? And if Woodrow Wilson had a dog like his old greyhound Mountain Boy around to console him for his shattered dream of a League of Nations, would he have died such a disappointed man? Doctors have long maintained that the simple act of petting a dog can reduce stress and lower high blood pressure — the problems that brought on Wilson's stroke.

Traphes Bryant, the White House kennel keeper from the time

of Harry Truman until Richard Nixon's resignation, maintained that dogs have enabled our presidents to keep a better perspective on life, and have even made it easier for them to win friends for the country, to say nothing of helping them win elections.

For five years Bill Clinton chose to overlook the benefits of a canine companion. Perhaps allergies caused him to bolt the White House door to dogs. But his personal physician made no mention of animal hair in diagnosing Clinton's chronic hoarseness and nasal congestion. In any case, if he were allergic to furry creatures, wouldn't Socks the cat have kept him coughing and sneezing?

In May 1993 he made a half-hearted attempt to buy a dog. It was during a benefit auction for the Sidwell Friends School in Washington, which his daughter Chelsea attended. The President offered $3,500 for a young golden retriever but bowed out of the bidding when the price hit $3,700. Just think, a few bucks more and that golden might have gotten in some good licks during the 1996 presidential campaign.

However, after being *cat*apulted, one could say, back into the White House for a second term with only feline support, Bill Clinton finally perked up his ears and welcomed a new First Dog, Buddy.

BELATED FIRST DOG

The young male chocolate Lab, named Buddy after the President's
great-uncle Henry "Buddy" Grisham, didn't realize all the state and
personal secrets he would be privy to when he got the run of the Oval
Office. During Clinton's impeachment trial it was said that Buddy
appeared to be "leakproof." Sadly, after leaving the safety of the
White House, Buddy was killed by a car near the Clintons' home
in Chappaqua, New York, in 2002.

The White House

★ ★ ★

After his mother's springer spaniel, Millie, had become such a White House celebrity and best-selling author as well, nobody expected George W. Bush to arrive dogless at 1600 Pennsylvania Avenue. Indeed he didn't. After his squeaker victory over Al Gore in the contentious 2000 election, he brought along a very senior First Dog already familiar with all the nooks and crannies of the presidential mansion. You see, Spot, a surviving brown and white daughter of Millie, had been born there.

Spot Fletcher, as she was officially named (after Scott Fletcher, the shortstop on the Texas Rangers baseball team W. owned before he became governor of Texas), didn't have the White House all to herself. Barney, a frisky Scottish terrier puppy, a gift from former Environmental Protection Agency chief Christine Todd Whitman, also moved in with the Bushes and quickly stole the show.

Barney became an instant movie star on the White House Web site. In subsequent so-called Barney Cams, he appeared on You Tube with country singer Dolly Parton, British prime minister Tony Blair, and in-house players including political adviser Karl Rove and White House chief of staff Andrew Card Jr. Released during the Christmas holiday seasons, the shows attracted millions of viewers from all over the world. But back home, sadly for

VIP TREATMENT

A Marine guard stands at attention as springer spaniel Spot and
Scottish terrier Barney step off a helicopter that flew them back to
the White House after a July 4th holiday celebration in Maine.
George W. Bush once called First Dog Barney "the son I never had."
They frequently played ball together on the White House lawn. Spot,
a daughter of the famous Millie, was born in the White House during
George H. W. Bush's presidency and died there during W.'s first term.

AP Images/Doug Mills/The White House

* * *

BAWLING OUT BARNEY

President Bush often kneeled down in the Oval Office to talk to
Barney on his own level, or occasionally to scold him. Shortly before
leaving the White House, Bush reprimanded him for napping while
the rest of the First Family was hurrying to vacate the premises. The
normally good-natured Scottie seemed to suffer from the Republicans'
loss of the 2008 election. Or perhaps he was just tired of being made
over by the press. Twice during the fall of 2008 he snarled
and bit members of the media who bent over to pet him.

AP Images/The White House

★ ★ ★

Barney, his pal Spot was put to sleep at the ripe old age of fifteen, leaving India the cat as his only four-footed playmate.

Barney became Bush's constant companion. Democrats claimed Bush clung to the dog because his poll ratings were sinking. As the war in Iraq dragged on, it was said that Barney became the President's own WMD, or in this case, "weapon of mass distraction." Critics claimed Bush was using Barney to divert attention from the Iraq mess the same way Clinton had used Buddy to divert attention from the scandal created by his trysts with White House intern Monica Lewinsky.

Beginning in 2005 Barney wasn't exactly demoted to Second Dog, but he had to share the White House stage with a fluffy little female Scottish terrier presented by Bush to the First Lady as a birthday present. They named the pup Miss Beazley, rather oddly it seemed, for Uncle Beazley, a dinosaur in Oliver Butterworth's children's book *The Enormous Egg*. Immediately, the pup started enjoying house privileges never extended to Barney. As Laura explained: "The President still gets up most mornings and brings me coffee. Now he comes in with Miss Beazley. She spends a little time running around the bed and jumping on us."

Maybe it was this new competition for the First Family's affection. Or perhaps it was the losing battle waged by the Republicans in the 2008 election campaign. In any case the good-natured Barney lost his temper a couple of times. In September when Heather Walker, public relations director of the Boston Celtics basketball team, bent down to pet him, Barney chomped on her wrist, sending her to the Celtics team physician's office for bandaging.

Two days after Republican John McCain lost to Barack Obama, Barney lost his cool once again. This time he vented his anger on Jon Decker, a Reuters TV correspondent who also tried to pet him. Barney snarled and bit Decker's right index finger, causing minor bleeding and the need for a tetanus shot.

In the hubbub of moving shortly before the Bushes vacated the White House, the President caught Barney sleeping during the day. "We're sprintin' to the finish, not nappin' to the finish," the President admonished. Barney slunk away, sensing that he was about to leave the fanciest dog house in America.

From the moment of Barack Obama's victory, experts weighed in with suggestions of various breeds for the new First Family. There appeared to be more qualified canine candidates than political candidates in the 2008 election campaign, and never before had the country gone so agog, and for so long, over the selection of a First Dog. The President called the choice "a major

BO'S PUBLIC DEBUT

With microphones thrust at him for the first time in his young life, America's newest First Dog failed to bark out any kind of an acceptance doggerel. Instead young Bo just licked the mike and ignored the hundred or so reporters and photographers present. The white-pawed Portuguese water dog puppy is going to need rigorous exercise in and out of the water to keep fit. The breed was originally used by fishermen in Portugal to catch fish and to dive to retrieve broken nets. Chip Somodevilla/Getty Images

* * *

IN TOW WITH THE FIRST FAMILY

Malia Obama, the President's ten-year-old daughter, takes a trial spin with Bo on the South Lawn of the White House, as her seven-year-old sister, Sasha, awaits her turn to hold the leash. Because of Malia's allergies, the President and First Lady (left) took special care to find a non-shedding breed. Bo was a gift from Senator Ted Kennedy and his wife, who own three Portuguese water dogs, including Bo's brother. Doug Mills/*The New York Times*/Redux

★ ★ ★

issue" in the Obama household, and a "hot topic" on his Web site. Not even the financial panic caused by the collapsing banks and company bailouts or the escalating war in Afghanistan could keep the choice of a First Dog out of the news.

And rightly so. When the much-heralded pooch finally entered the White House the weight of history would fall on its haunches, just as it did on Warren Harding's airedale Laddie Boy, who attended cabinet meetings seated in his own hand-carved chair, and on Franklin Roosevelt's Scottish terrier Fala, who witnessed the signing of the Atlantic Charter with Winston Churchill aboard the USS *Augusta*. And those two famous presidential pals were no exceptions. From George Washington's favorite fox-hound Tipler to George W. Bush's beloved Scottie Barney, First Dogs have played an important political role.

At first Obama seemed to favor an underdog. He mentioned the possibility of canvassing canine shelters for a mixed breed, or as he put it, for a "mutt like me." But then because of ten-year-old daughter Malia's allergies the family narrowed the field to two "hypoallergenic" non-shedders, a Labradoodle (part Labra-dor retriever, part poodle), and a Portuguese water dog. "This has been tougher than finding a commerce secretary," Obama confessed to George Stephanopoulos on the ABC News program

This Week. But let's face it, all the speculation provided a little doggone fun at a somber period when it was badly needed.

As the whole world now knows, the final vote went to a Portuguese water dog. Known for centuries along Portugal's coast as *cao de agua* (dog of water), the breed is strong, smart, and loyal, and according to the American Kennel Club, has "the ability to swim all day." The dogs accompanied Portuguese fishermen and were used for diving for fish and for retrieving broken nets, as well as for carrying messages between boats. Their tails, added the AKC, can be "carried gallantly" high on land, or used as a rudder down in the water, a feature hardly necessary for navigating in the confines of the White House pool.

The choice of a "Portie," as these water dogs are called, was backed by Senator Ted Kennedy, who owns a lively trio named Sunny, Splash, and Cappy. When he and his wife, Victoria, discovered that their breeder had a six-month-old black and white brother of Cappy named Charlie available, they purchased him as a present for the President's two daughters. Actually, the pup's registered AKC name was Amigo's New Hope. The girls promptly rechristened the dog Bo, not after the President's initials as some wag claimed but after a cousin's cat named Bo, and Mrs. Obama's father who was nicknamed Diddley, after the legendary musician Bo Diddley.

As a swarm of reporters and photographers followed the new First Dog's initial public romp around the White House South Lawn, the animal right's activists began carping that the President had scuttled his original plan to get a homeless mutt from a canine shelter. But in a way Bo could be considered homeless, having been returned to the breeder because he didn't get along with the previous owner's other dog.

Despite his celebrity status, Bo was bred as a work dog and will need to be given vigorous daily exercise, both in and out of the water. Perhaps the President will swim with him in the White House pool as John Kennedy did with daughter Caroline's Welsh terrier, Charlie, and Lyndon Johnson did with his adopted stray mutt, Yuki. In any case, when Bo is finally unleashed and given the run of the grounds, he will be able to cool off on hot summer days under the fountains behind the White House as Gerald Ford's golden retriever Liberty liked to do. Asked by a reporter whether Bo will be privy to meetings in the Oval Office as most of his predecessors were, the President replied, "Of course." And where will Bo sleep? "Not in my bed," declared the leader of the free world.

Wherever he sleeps, whether it's in a fancily furnished dog-house outside, as did Ronald Reagan's Cavalier King Charles spaniel Rex, or in the room with Malia or Sasha, Bo will surely

HEADING FOR THE OVAL OFFICE

Pete Souza/The White House

* * *

ACKNOWLEDGMENTS

THE AUTHORS ARE DEEPLY GRATEFUL TO THE FOLLOWING INDIVIDUALS AND ORGANIZATIONS. We would have been in the doghouse without their help in gathering the research and locating the pictures used in this book.

Our special thanks to Barbara Kolk, librarian at the American Kennel Club headquarters in New York City, whose tireless digging enabled us to uncover pictures and information buried deeper than a retriever's bone.

For their dogged perseverance we would also like to thank the Library of Congress; the New York Public Library; the Mount Vernon Ladies' Association; the Library Department of Mount Vernon; Celeste Walker, associate editor of *The Adams Papers*, Massachusetts Historical Society; the Thomas Jefferson Memorial Foundation, Inc.; Montpelier, home of James Madison; James Wootton, curator at Ash Lawn–Highland, home of James

Monroe; the James Monroe Museum and Memorial Library; the Hermitage, home of Andrew Jackson; the Tennessee State Library and Archives; the Indiana Historical Society; the James Polk Ancestral Library; the Kentucky Historical Society; Lindenwald, home of Martin Van Buren; the Filson Club Historical Society; the Penfield Library, State University of New York College at Oswego; the Buffalo & Erie Historical Society Library; the Bowdoin College Library; the Dickinson College Library; Wheatland, home of James Buchanan; the Illinois State Historical Library; U.S. National Park Service, the Andrew Johnson Historic Site Library; the University of Tennessee; the New York Historical Society; the Rutherford B. Hayes Presidential Center; the Lake County (Ohio) Historical Society; Hiram College Library; the President Benjamin Harrison Home; the McKinley Museum of History, Science & Industry; the Harvard College Library; the Oyster Bay Historical Society (New York); the U.S. National Park Service, William Howard Taft Historic Site Library; the Princeton University Firestone Library; Arthur S. Link, editor, *The Papers of Woodrow Wilson*; Woodrow Wilson House/National Trust; the Ohio Hisorical Society; the National Museum of American History, Smithsonian Institution; the Forbes Library/Coolidge Collection, Northampton, Massachusetts; the Herbert Hoover Library; the Franklin D. Roosevelt Library; the

FDR Memorial Commission; the Harry S Truman Library; the Dwight D. Eisenhower Library; the John F. Kennedy Library; the Lyndon Baines Johnson Library; the Richard Nixon Materials Project, National Archives; the Richard Nixon Library & Birthplace; the Gerald R. Ford Library; the Jimmy Carter Library; the Ronald Reagan Library; the Bush Presidential Library; Philip B. Kunhardt, Jr.; Valerie Doyle and Maxie; William Morrow & Co.; UPI/Corbis-Bettmann; the Associated Press; and Time-Life Editorial Services.

We are also doggone grateful to our agent Carol Mann and to our good friend Robbin Reynolds. They showed our proposal to publisher Elisabeth Scharlatt at Algonquin Books of Chapel Hill, who with seeing-eye perspicacity passed it on to editor Robert Rubin. Fortunately, he kept us on a tight leash, all the while strengthening these pages with a little kibble of his own. We are also grateful to Algonquin's Brunson Hoole and Anne Winslow.

And for this updated edition, special thanks to Bobbi Baker Burrows, Life Books Director of Photography, and Russell Burrows.

ABOUT THE AUTHORS

ROY ROWAN has been a correspondent and editor for *Life, Time,* and *Fortune* and has contributed to other major magazines. He is the author of numerous books and articles on business, foreign affairs, and politics, including *The Intuitive Manager, Powerful People,* and *Chasing the Dragon,* which is being made into a movie by Universal Pictures. He lives in Greenwich, Connecticut.

BROOKE JANIS worked for years as a television producer at CBS News and other national media. She lives in New York City.